A Break in M

C000110017

This is CARL IGOLEN-ROBINSON's first book. The idea to put his son's story down in writing first came to him after a chance meeting with a friend in the fixtures and fittings aisle of a DIY shop. When asked by his friend what his news was, Carl told the story. By the time he'd finished, his friend was in tears. Decision made; the story needed to be shared!

Carl is donating 100% of his royalties of the sale of this book to the RFU Injured Players Foundation.

To Ben

Carl Robinson

Carl Igolen-Robinson

A Break in Mendoza

A Break in Mendoza
Written by Carl Igolen-Robinson

ISBN: 978-1-912243-77-8

Printed Edition
Also available in multiple e-book formats.

Published by
The Endless Bookcase Ltd, Suite 14 STANTA Business Centre,
3 Soothouse Spring, St Albans, Hertfordshire, AL3 6PF, UK.

More information can be found at
www.theendlessbookcase.com.

This book is dedicated to the good people of

Los Tordos Rugby Club, Mendoza, Argentina

and special thanks to

Angus MacDonald
Celeste Igolen-Robinson
Cesar Dalla Torre
Enrique "Pitu" Molina Lera
Francisco "Pancho" Herrera
Haileybury & Imperial Service College
Howard Holdsworth
Jim Hounsell
John Hargreaves
Jonathan George
Juan Francisco Aliaga
Julio "Tano" Cabrero
Mr Ahmed & The Princess Alexandra Hospital, Harlow
Mr Terraza & La Clinica Francesa
The RFU Injured Players Foundation
Will Carling
Will Greenwood
Will Mould

About the Author

Born in Brighton in 1973, from a French mother and English father, Carl Igolen-Robinson was first educated at St. Christopher's School, Hove before spending seven years at Christ's Hospital. He read European Studies at Royal Holloway, London University before completing a PGCE in French and PE at Homerton College, Cambridge. Married with two sons, Carl has been an educator all his life teaching French and coaching cricket and rugby. His pastoral role as a leader in the boarding environment has given him most satisfaction, with tutees and boys in his house giving him regular cause to praise. He finds watching them grow into young men of fine character hugely rewarding and playing a guiding part in that journey a genuine privilege.

His other loves include his friends, family, cooking (preferably for others), films, drawing, gardening and he has a particular enthusiasm for lawn care.

Contents

Foreword

Rugby for me is the ultimate invasion game, though it is far more than an organised collection of players tasked with carrying a ball over a line. For a game with such an apparently basic objective, it possesses such tactical and technical complexities as to likely baffle any onlooker with no experience of the sport. One can dissect the game itself with its set pieces and flowing, often creative and aesthetically pleasing loose play in fine detail; the balance between attacking play and often brutal, steadfast and at times highly structured defence. However, rooted in the very soul of this sport, which underpin everything that players and coaches wish to achieve, are human values such as trust, collective and individual responsibility, discipline and loyalty. In addition, there is an immediately identifiable and particular social aspect to rugby that is common to players of all ages and levels. It's a culture utterly conducive to building friendships for life. Whether you're a grassroots player operating on a muddy backfield of a local club, with its fading pitch markings and corner flags which *"won't put themselves away"*, or a Rugby World Cup winner, more at home entertaining thousands in tall, imposing stadia on the global rugby theatre, the common social bond enjoyed by all players is hugely tangible. It's born from a shared understanding whereby you will put your body on the line for your best pals, and a culture of honesty and solidarity when facing the inevitable challenges of adversity, be that away at Old Somethingonians in the local merit table or facing the All Blacks at Eden Park. As a rugby player, wherever you go in the world, you can be sure of a warm welcome, an invitation to come training with the promise of a loan of some old kit, or simply an opportunity to share a beer and talk about the game. What is abundantly clear from this story, is that such values of the game are surviving, alive and well, all over the world, and not just a flashback to an amateur era resonating here and there in the modern game. The support that Luke and his father received during the challenging times described in this book is testament to that.

Injuries come with rugby; it's a brutal, physical sport. However, these days, more than ever, the emphasis on correctly preparing players of all ages both physically and mentally for the impacts and collisions of the sport has been pushed to the very forefront of the agenda. Despite measures being in place for the prevention of injuries, they do happen. It's then down to medical teams and individuals to ensure the correct steps are in place to rest, recover and return. It is rarely a process carried out individually and alone.

It is reassuring to sense the ongoing theme of widespread, caring and effective support as this story unfolds: the immediate actions of the club doctor; the unconditional and vital support of members of Los Tordos Rugby Club; the surprise appearance of international players; the ongoing assistance by Jonathan George; and of course the faultless support of friends and family all remotely monitored by the Injured Players Foundation (IPF) at the RFU.

The story is a timely reminder to us all that if you set your mind to a goal, with the right levels of determination, help and assistance, time and the environment in which to operate, anything is possible. Luke attacked his own personal challenge head-long, showing great courage and maturity beyond his years. I am delighted that his father thought to put down in words this inspirational record of Luke's year-long challenge and to publish it in support of the IPF. Their unbelievable work up and down the country, in support of players who have suffered serious injury, and who have been less fortunate than Luke, is extremely worthy of all our support. On that basis, I hope the book is a real success.

By Will Greenwood

How it Kicks Off

Like lots of fathers, I used to observe my son Luke (our second) in the garden as a toddler, picking balls up of various sizes and shapes. He would run this way and that and was fairly successful when it came to kicking a ball around. He loved sport from the outset and the moment he could join our local rugby club, Hertford RFC in the minis' section as a five-year-old, he did. Luke had been around the hundred percentile for height and weight since birth and he seemed destined to make an impact on the rugby field. Sadly, until contact was introduced in the U9s, he had to settle for having more fleet-footed, speedy scamps hurtling round him like fireflies. Moving up through the year groups he developed well at his school, Haileybury, where Saracens Internationals Jamie George, Nick Isiekwe and Chris Wyles had once honed their skills. Under the guidance of the Director of Rugby, former British Lion Michael Owen, he improved his skill set alongside his physical potential. In cup competitions, he would play for the year above and never appeared out of place, indeed he would make valuable contributions. So when his Housemaster Matt Radley (a colleague and friend) approached me in the Common Room to say that a place on the senior tour to South America the following summer had come up for Luke, we were all very excited. Despite the fact that he would be the second youngest on the trip, I had no concerns thanks to his size and to his successful and enjoyable experiences playing for the year above.

The cost of the tour was an eye-watering £2500, which even given months of advance notice to save up, was an unrealistic figure for us as a family. I communicated this to Matt Radley who was down to lead the tour aided by three colleagues. He said he would approach The Master, Mr Collier as in the past, pupils who were not necessarily financially able to make the most of such opportunities had been supported from a discretionary fund. Not long afterwards, I had a one-to-one conversation with The Master who agreed to provide a £1000 towards the cost of this tour on the condition that on his return, Luke made arrangements to meet with Mr Collier to discuss the tour in person. When the time came of course, nearly a year later, Luke had that meeting with The Master, but the conversation turned out to be predominantly about Luke's near catastrophic injury. It was, more importantly, about the extraordinary human experience that we both shared in Mendoza - an unforgettable story of rugby camaraderie and solidarity, unconditional assistance, of new friendships alongside medical wizardry and an ongoing outpouring of care and support.

Not long after Luke's confirmation on the tour, Matt Radley was successful in getting a promotion in another school and he approached me to replace him on the tour. During the previous April I had been on the 1st XI cricket tour to India and had experienced such a fantastic trip that I didn't hesitate for a moment to take up the opportunity. I suppose it was also a good chance to follow Luke's progress and to keep a fatherly eye on him, although I must confess that I didn't communicate that to anyone, especially Luke! Outwardly, I was simply doing my duty as an experienced Haileybury rugby coach!

Luke attended all the summer warm-up training that took place with great relish. I occasionally wandered out to the playing fields to watch, resisting the temptation to join in, in the heat, sweat and hard ground! Preparations were going well and Luke's grandparents had also offered £500 for us as spending money during the tour which was a real boost. We had much to look forward to and the tour as a whole, would be a great experience, allowing Luke to develop as a player and as a person, perhaps even giving him more chance of breaking into the Saracens Junior Academy the following season.

That was the hope.

<u>14th August 2018, off to South America.</u>

On arrival at Heathrow airport, there was the usual bustling around waiting for players to arrive in dribs and drabs. I remember being struck by how brave a couple of the boys had been. Two boys new into the Lower Sixth had signed up to the tour and were therefore meeting everyone for the first time. I remember being really impressed with Zach and Cameron; "fair play for taking the plunge", I remember thinking. Then again, joining a group of rugby players on a tour ought to be a pretty comfortable way of settling in to a new school! And so it would turn out. We were spread out rather sensibly, all over this enormous plane. We had readied ourselves for the 14.5 hour flight, renowned as British Airways' longest flight – Heathrow to Santiago in Chile. The airline had made a few accommodations in terms of comfort even in economy and it was certainly better than I was used to, popping backwards and forwards to France as I do, on well-known *no-frills* airlines. However, economy it was! I remember dropping in on Luke a few times during the flight in an attempt to encourage him to get some sleep. I was clearly wasting my time as he was predictably glued to the various media offerings and film selection being beamed at him from the small screen just a few inches from his face. When I suggested he should recline his seat and get some *shuteye,* he moaned abruptly to me that his seat would not recline… with the kind of sharpness only teenagers use with their parents. That said, I did sympathise and went directly to the staff pleading for a solution. 14.5 hours on a seat that did not recline struck me as the kind of torturous exercise that would not look out of place in a late 60s James Bond film, with Sean Connery strapped in, and a well-dressed villain looking on. Luke's bad luck of having the only seat on the plane that didn't recline quickly flipped and rather than flick an annoyingly concealed switch that neither of us had seen in order to fix the seat, Luke was hoiked out of economy and upgraded to premium economy! Luke made no attempt to conceal his glee as not only did he move up to premium economy, he was personally settled in to one of those seats at the front with the extra legroom. This, for a 6'3" 15-year-old, was an absolute result! As it would turn out, it was not the last time in this story that I would suffer Luke's gratuitous gloating on the back of a British Airways upgrade!

On our arrival in Chile, we met our local guide for the first time. He was a rather diminutive figure, very casually dressed who introduced himself as Pitu, which he explained was a nickname meaning *Smurf.* That Pitu looked like he had slept in his clothes that night, and only for a few hours, mattered not as there was a warmth to this man that was evident from the moment we first shook hands. Pitu had played a little rugby himself and was a genial host and incredibly easy to get on with. We arrived early in the morning and few could resist the predictable jokes about how chilly Chile was. As is often the case when touring, the first coach journey to the hotel was a real eye-opener as we made our way through some incredibly poor areas and frequent cultural reminders of how lucky we all are to live where we do and as we do. When we de-bussed in front of our hotel we were greeted from across the road by a local ne'er-do-well shrieking over at us with his chums in a language none of us understood. Therefore, his insults and threats were totally wasted on us; a fact that I don't think this chap's tiny and underused brain had calculated. However, when he issued the internationally recognisable cutthroat gesture, pulling his thumb across his throat from one ear to the other with a huge grin on his face, nodding slightly, communication had been successfully achieved! We would give these guys a wide berth! "Welcome to Santiago" I thought.

Santiago itself was fascinating with a deep history and two very clear areas: one rather rundown and the other very modern and progressive. Everywhere you got the sense that Chile was modelling itself on the United States, though quite why was a concept that evaded us all. The beauty of the Andes that seemed to surround us was breath taking and certainly a memorable sight. After various guided tours and meals our focus moved to the rugby and with only a day or so before our first game it was important to set up a training session. Staggeringly, it seemed we were to have to pay a huge amount to hire a ground and not only that, but also additional coach costs to travel there, so we set about exploring the possibility of using one of the many local parks for our session. After not too long we found a beautiful spot, walked the ground to assess the possibilities and planned a session for the next day. We had a really purposeful session despite the heat and the long walk to and from the underground station (an episode we had negotiated successfully without losing a single young Englishman to the Santiago Metro system!). With 35 players on the tour, and only four games scheduled, there was a lot of pressure on me as the head coach to ensure all the players returned home with enough game time under their belts and that the appropriate quality of player would be selected in light of the opposition. When on tour, this is easier said than done as often little is known about the opponents. It was up to Pitu to give us the intel on the oppo. He assured us that Santiago College, our first and only game in Chile would be our weakest opponents on tour. I carefully sat down and planned a 2nd XV line up, based largely on Michael Owen's suggestions. Game one, at Santiago College surrounded by the extraordinary Chilean landscape was a total mismatch. According to Pitu remember, they would be "the weakest team". Their international fly-half set the tone from the start and it was an uncomfortable exercise for the Haileybury team. Players who had been U16B and even C teamers the previous season, stepped up and showed incredible spirit, courage and resilience. With some appropriate shifting of personnel on both teams, the second half was far more competitive. However, the afternoon had been testing to say the least. The highlight of the day was a very pleasant and unrushed lunch, hosted by Santiago College. In an extraordinary gesture of generous hosting, a female member of staff, whose name now evades me, whose job it was to ensure the smooth running of the college's daily operations, came over to the staff table to announce she would drum up a few female pupils to entertain our boys. My first impression was that this was a deliberate attempt to throw the boys mentally prior to the match! As it turned out, some of these young ladies seemed to need no encouragement from this nice staff member and were fascinated by our chaps, though once again I was baffled as to why. Astonishingly, some of the boys approached us to say they would like to attend the afternoon's first lesson alongside their new Chilean female friends, having been invited. While I enjoyed the rare enthusiasm for attending lessons, all the staff unanimously agreed that this would be a potentially calamitous course of action! We left Santiago College a little bruised but with no significant injuries and much to discuss with our tour guide Pitu, who announced on the coach on the way back to the hotel "I was really surprised! They had a good team!"

I didn't warm hugely to Santiago, although I know Luke really enjoyed his time there and as a rugby experience it left a little to be desired. I couldn't wait, however, to hop over the Andes and arrive in Argentina. First stop, Mendoza! I knew very little about Mendoza other than it was the home of excellent red wine and the best steaks in the world! None of us could wait frankly.

Arriving in Mendoza

The plane journey from Santiago to Mendoza was exactly what one might consider to be a short hop. No sooner had we reached cruising altitude, then we were starting our descent. Sadly for us on this occasion, it was something of a gloomy day and low cloud ruined what would otherwise have been a quite spectacular view as we hopped over the Andes. We caught a decent glimpse of the lower peaks just prior to disappearing up into the clouds, but it only served to press home how we had really missed out. I confess that I spent much of the flight thinking of that extraordinary film "Alive", which tells the true story of a South American rugby team who crashed into the Andes. A handful survived the ordeal after the shocking but inevitable and ultimately wise decision to begin feeding on their dead and frozen teammates. We landed safely in Mendoza having successfully avoided the mountain range, much to my relief.

Yet again, our first flavour of the region was experienced through the reinforced glass windows of our coach. Between the airport and city there was much evidence of an agricultural tradition but even on this side of the Andes we were not spared the sight of real poverty. All along the main road were dotted huge piles of litter and various styles and designs of improvised shacks where one presumed some poor souls called home. Eventually we arrived in the city centre of Mendoza. Mendoza is a rather flat, sprawled out city, and its centre seems a real middle-class cocoon with its magnificent steak restaurants, hotels and banks. We checked into a rather fancy hotel and on this occasion were greeted with nothing but warmth. The lack of any yobs on street corners threatening to cut our throats was comfortingly reassuring! "This was more like it," I thought.

Pitu, an Argentinian from Buenos Aires, was clearly very excited to now be hosting us properly in his own country. I'd lost count of the number of times he mentioned that we would be going to a steak restaurant on our first night. Oh boy, he did not let us down! We went to a restaurant called *Focunda*. Inside we found two or three gentlemen in their 50s, absolutely immaculately dressed in a tidily kept, warm and friendly restaurant. The moment I walked in I got the sense we were in for a real treat. 35 teenage boys, 4 visiting coaches and 1 very excited and proud tour guide, were seated at various tables with the minimum of fuss. After a fabulous starter of local sausages and accompaniments, the main event: 40 steaks, the size and flavour of which were absolutely mind blowing, were expertly delivered in timely fashion alongside bowls of chips. This was also served with a beautiful salad (one of the last we would see on the trip !!). The restaurant fell near silent as the chomping began. To our great surprise and delight, Pitu announced that this had been the restaurant at which his family and friends had eaten the night of his wedding. In fact, where the staff had settled in, table 11, had been the exact table he and his new wife, along with close family, had sat that night. We all thought that was very special. For those that still had room, a beautiful locally made ice cream dessert with a huge bowl of "dulce de leche" was next up. This irresistible, moreish home-made gooey caramel will stick in my mind for some time. I freely admit to having *overdone it* massively on the "dulce de leche"! While the food was delicious, it was my and Luke's first taste of Mendocino warmth and hospitality. What's more, Pitu was really growing on me as a human being.

Our first full day in Mendoza turned out to be exactly that - FULL! In the evening we were set to arrive at Los Tordos Rugby Club, where our players would be billeted out in ones and twos to various families and parents of the players we would play against the following day. It was something the staff were looking forward to as on such occasions, it's possible to relax a little in the evening. However, before any of that could happen, we had the small matter of a trip to the mountains with zip-lining and white water rafting to negotiate.

We had about an hour and a half journey on the coach to arrive in the mountains. On the way we took in a great deal of the countryside. I was quite struck by the dryness and desert-like feel of the area. Huge wide-open spaces punctuated with mountains made the whole area look much like parts of Arizona which many would recognise from much loved westerns. Indeed, everywhere I looked, it seemed likely that at any moment, Clint Eastwood might appear from behind a pile of boulders on a trusty *"I don't think it's nice you laughing"* mule. There was Tumbleweed amongst mini canyons and I dare say a few rattlesnakes to boot! Much of the flat areas, however, were populated with vast vineyards as far as the eye could see; mostly, I was reliably told, growing my favourite grape variety – Malbec. When we parked up at this adventure centre in the mountains, we were greeted by members of the family that had run it for decades. Everybody seemed to know everybody and we were first made to feel very welcome before the plan of action was spelled out. It would be zip-lining first, then a spot of lunch followed by the white-water rafting. Lunch by the way, we could already see cooking in the big open barbecue over in the corner of the room. About 40 chickens roasting away slowly! I knew it was going to be awesome. The only snag that I could see was that it was absolutely freezing! We put on our various harnesses, hardhats and leather gloves and stood in a straight line in front of this no-nonsense lady, who struck me as the kind of character that would tame the liveliest of classrooms. I've heard a number of similar safety briefs during my time involved with the cadet forces and this one was spot on. Direct and clear and rather amusingly from my point of view, her management of boys *and staff* who were not paying attention during her brief was equally direct. Off we went in a queue going one at a time down these zip lines. For anyone who has not experienced this kind of activity, you effectively hook yourself onto a thick wire suspended between point A and point B, point A being higher than point B and thus, once released, you hurtle from point A to point B, with Sir Isaac Newton and his views on gravity very much in charge! In order to slow down, we had been reliably informed during our safety brief that one simply pulls down on the wire. Seemed easy enough! We started off on something of a baby zip line. No more I would think than about 70 m. This I guessed was our practice run. 20 or so of the boys managed with great success and it was all quite amusing and entertaining. However, one young man in our group, more of the 'prop' variety than the 'wing' variety shall we say, got himself in a complete tangle halfway down. Spinning round a couple of times, losing grip with his leather gloved hand thus incapable of doing the braking thing, he clattered into the other side of the mountain taking the member of staff with him. For a moment, arms, heads and legs were flying in all directions and for a split second it was impossible to distinguish which body parts belonged to our player and which belonged to the member of staff. Eventually, all movement ceased, the two bodies became disentangled and normal service was resumed. He was a bit shaken, given a telling off, which we all thought was a little harsh, and sent on his way down the next zip-line. This next one was certainly not a practice one: it looked about 500 metres long as it disappeared off and down into the distance where we could see tiny versions of our players successfully slowing before reaching the lower platform. Great fun!

I was at the back with my good friend and colleague Jon Medcraft, a wily and supremely experienced Welshman who headed up our Economics Department. Like many Welshman, Jon is a fantastic storyteller and a rugby fanatic from the toes up; one of life's really genuine chaps and utterly likeable. Earlier, he'd made me laugh properly out loud. "Watching these guys hurtling down the line has reminded me of a saying" he said to me: "*If you can keep your head, while all around are losing theirs......you obviously haven't grasped the gravity of the situation!*" The weather was worsening and as we queued for the last absolutely enormous zip-line that crossed the river at its widest point. The female instructor, who had been charming the pants off us all as we waited (I do hope that translates appropriately into Spanish), explained that because of the crosswind, the lighter people may struggle to go all away to the end. In this event, we'd have to pull ourselves along on the last bit. I quickly suggested that perhaps she and I could double up making up the weight and increasing our chances of a successful arrival. An innocent enough suggestion completely taken the wrong way by all those around! That's my recollection anyhow. Jon and I were having a good chuckle about it at the back of the queue. We were the last two to go and to my absolute delight, the instructor turned and said, "Come on, let's double up and get across". Delight turned to disgust as I noticed she was talking to Jon. I couldn't believe my suggestion had been taken up and literally stolen by my buddy, though to be fair it wasn't his fault. Having never attempted such an operation Jon asked, "So how is this going to work?" She replied, "Don't worry, I'll just grip you between my thighs." Jon didn't stop laughing for about 24 hours. She left me to go last and I watched her and Jon disappear down the zip-line, the two of them held together by exactly what she'd promised - a firm grip between her legs. I made it across just fine by myself and had lunch to look forward to. It turned out to be a total treat: the roasted chicken, vegetables, potatoes, accompanied by delicious empanadas, small pastry parcels not unlike our own Cornish pasties only smaller and frankly tastier (at this point I think it would be wise and prudent to apologise to any readers from the Independent Republic of Cornwall).

We had one lad with concussion and it was decided he would not do the white water rafting along with a young man who claimed he suffered terribly with seasickness. A moment of mental weakness which I'm not proud of, led me to suggest I would stay behind and supervise these two boys, as members of the public were around and the lads might be at risk. In the back of my mind I knew there must be some policy in some document back at school, the conditions of which I would be entirely satisfying with this decision. In truth, I didn't fancy stripping down, sticking on an ill-fitting wetsuit and paddling down a freezing cold river, essentially melted ice from the mountains, in freezing cold windy conditions. I sat guiltily as the rest of the tour party set off in their inevitably unflattering wetsuits and helmets, in the freezing cold mountain air. I felt ashamed and that heavy feeling of guilt ran deep, deep within me for literally several minutes before I ordered my first hot chocolate!

Two hours later the lads returned and to a man, they were all a different colour from when last I had seen them: their shoulders were placed firmly somewhere near their ears, their elbows glued tightly to their rib cages and their arms crossed tightly across their chest, and at the end of these arms, only barely recognisable freezing cold purple hands, clenched tightly to show every sinew of their knuckles. They shivered their way to the changing rooms, then shivered their way to the holding area before shivering their way to the bar and decimating the entire world's supply of hot chocolate in moments. I remember thinking the bill for chocolate would likely mount up to more than we had paid for the rafting!

It had been a fantastic day and we trooped back to the bus looking forward to perhaps a little sleep as we made our way to Los Tordos Rugby Club, to arrange the billeting out of our boys to the LTRC players' homes and families. I can tell you the bus journey was pretty quiet as most had nodded off by the time we'd left the car park. So far Luke seemed to have been enjoying the tour and was mixing well with the older boys in the group. There was nothing remotely to suggest the kind of disaster that was now less than 24 hours away.

Billeting

It was dark by the time we arrived at Los Tordos Rugby Club. We had no idea what to expect from an Argentinian rugby club. Our first impression was a long noisy gravel drive at the end of which we could see the reassuring sight of a floodlit pitch with tall, proud rugby posts, brightly illuminated, poking up into the night sky. "Floodlights were already a good sign", I thought. As we drew nearer the pitch and car park it became clear that there wasn't a single blade of grass on this pitch; however, it was very flat and the lines were clearly marked out. We parked up, and began the process of heaving out all the boys' suitcases and kit bags from the belly of our coach before parading along a gravel path to the clubhouse. As we walked it was obvious that there was much more to LTRC than the rather bald floodlit pitch we had passed on the way in. It was a complex collection of rugby pitches, gym facilities, clubhouses and furthermore, a hockey club for good measure. Evidently, this was a serious set-up!

It was extremely cold. However, we received a warm welcome from a number of club officials and parents. As is often the case on such occasions, there was a group of Argentinian teenaged boys on one side of the terraced area to the front of the clubhouse, slightly cautiously eyeing up their new overseas opponents and on the other side, an anxious looking bunch of English boys. What could they expect? They were waiting to be assigned to a family they did not know, in a town they did not know and likely would need to communicate in a language they did not know. The only common ground it would seem, was a love for rugby and of course the fact that they were teenage boys! I recall thinking that the various X boxes and PlayStations would likely play a key part in breaking down barriers and our boys settling into their new homes where they would stay the next two nights. Judging by the photographs I received later in hospital on my phone, the lads wasted no time getting to know their host families and seemed to have had an absolute ball!

Two officials on that night stood out from the crowd. The team manager in charge of the U17 group was a chap called Tano. He seemed like a nice fellow though he spoke no English and despite this he was slowly but surely working his way down the list of players pairing them off efficiently with their Argentinian counterparts. Steadily, our group began to decrease in size as each one nervously shuffled towards his opponent and their parents who were doing their best to reassure and welcome with smiles, hugs and enthusiastic handshakes. I was struck by the effortless warmth of these *medocinos*.

The other official was the coach. There was a different feel to this chap who had a face that looked particularly lived in and he struck me as a rather uncompromising, dare I say, fearsome-looking chap. It was with him, via the assistance of Pitu and his language skills, that we began discussing the format of the next day's match. It wasn't long before we were discussing the prospect of playing two games back to back. It would take some planning in terms of personnel but they were proposing a 1st XV game followed by a 2nd XV game. They had a huge squad and all the boys had foregone departing on holiday in order to accommodate our visit. We agreed and later, I set about planning the two squads which would involve a large bench for the 1st XV, who might not necessarily get on but would certainly start the second game.

Luke had been paired up with a young lad called Tomi, who seemed like a nice fellow. I took the opportunity obviously, as Luke's Dad, to wander over and introduce myself to him. He appeared to be a warm and charming young man. The two of them headed off to Tomi's house driven by his older brother. There was nothing to indicate at that moment, to what extent Tomi and his family would shape the next fortnight of our lives.

Pitu was a great help in assisting Tano as we tried to make sense of the whole process and battled against our boys' natural tendency to stick together using the *safety in numbers* approach to dealing with an anxious situation. The mass of folks and the unmistakable sound of wheelie suitcases slowly dissipated but it did take a huge amount of time as some parents did not arrive till much later. It was our first taste of what we came to describe as *mendocino time;* essentially a pretty relaxed approach to punctuality! I made a mental note that we shouldn't get caught out the next day during the warm-up process; I would make a point of regularly making contact with the referee to confirm the kick-off time and how many minutes we would have left.

Finally, the courtyard was empty, we said our goodbyes to Tano and the scary coach and hopped back on our bus. We returned to the hotel looking forward to yet another steak supper that we had promised ourselves. That we were about two hours behind schedule was of no real concern as the boys were off our hands for the first time in days. It's an extraordinary feeling of relief and calmness that I think only someone who has experienced touring with pupils might understand fully.

We went to a different restaurant not far from where we had been the night before. It was very busy with a completely different, more lively atmosphere. The adult team sat around an immaculately laid table: our welsh Head of Economics Jon Medcraft, the Head of Psychology Angus MacDonald, the newly appointed Head of Strength & Conditioning, Joe Satt, Pitu and myself. It was another *protein fest* but this time we had been faced with the prospect of selecting from a menu we didn't understand. Pitu to the rescue as usual! Lovely food! Sumptuous Malbec! Fabulous company!

August 19th 2018

The next day the coaching team and Pitu arrived promptly at LTRC for an early afternoon kick-off. Now the club was bathed in sunlight and we could see it for what it was. What a fantastic place! We were to play on the 1st XV pitch and here, no issues with grass coverage! It was a beautiful emerald rectangle set amongst several brown, dusty practice pitches. There was a basic setup of tiered seating along both touchlines and advertising hoardings all around, giving yet more evidence that we were at a club of some significance. I later found out that the Argentinian scrum-half at the time, Gonzalo Bertranou, was a former player at Los Tordos.

Our strength and conditioning coach, Joe Satt, had recently joined the school from Exeter Chiefs. Joe had been a pupil at Haileybury during my time and it was a real delight to have him with us. He planned and ran an excellent warm-up and we kicked off on time *(more or less)*. The teams were really evenly matched which was a massive relief after the disaster in Santiago. Both teams played an expansive and ambitious brand of rugby which resulted in a handful of unbelievably good tries from distance involving several players, line-breaks and offloads. These were the kind of tries that both sets of supporters spontaneously applaud regardless of partisan tendencies! Great theatre!

Sadly, there was one potentially significant injury during the first half as our winger Jacob Suter had collapsed in a tackle and was evidently in significant pain. Los Tordos had a doctor on-site and it was not long before Jacob was being taken off to hospital for various tests and no doubt x-rays. Angus set off with Jacob and Pitu in the ambulance.

Luke had been on the bench for this first game and was given the last 15 min in order to gain some experience at that level but would start in the second game. After another good warm-up, the second game began and while it was clear the home team were a little stronger, our 2nd XV played with great spirit and were achieving a good deal more gain-line success and ball retention than was the case in Chile. Luke found himself in open play chasing down a centre who had made a line-break. He made a successful tackle, the ball was recycled and play moved on. Initially, as the coach, I followed the play but soon became aware that Luke had not risen from the tackle area. I had been watching Luke playing rugby since he was six so I wasn't immediately alarmed to see that he might have picked up some kind of knock. Joe was in assistance and the club doctor was once again very quickly on the scene. In these scenarios involving Luke, I have always taken the view that I should stand back and let those who are there to manage these situations get on with it, give them space and not hover around getting stressed or worse, stressing Luke out. I remained therefore on the touchline for some time, clutching my coach's clipboard and stopwatch, and following the game. I didn't wander far and

I kept an eye on the unfolding situation in our 22, as medical staff were crouching around my son.

As I continued to glance over, I did become more and more anxious as I saw no obvious movement from Luke and the doctor was now kneeling with his hands either side of Luke's head, gently holding it still. I was conscious at that time that this resembled a scene I'd seen on so many rugby fields both in front of my very own eyes or indeed on the television. The words of so many commentators were echoing in my head: "this is just a precaution". It's a phrase that anyone who has watched a good deal of rugby has heard on many occasions. Indeed, in a similar situation almost exactly a year before, in a game at Hertford RFC, Luke had made a try-saving tackle 5 m from his own goal-line, against strong rivals Bishops Stortford in the dying minutes of a close game. It was identical in many ways; an ambulance arrived, the neck brace was fitted, he was cautiously manoeuvred onto the spinal board and carted off to the Princess Alexandra Hospital in Harlow. "It's just a precaution" I was told and indeed I was reasonably relaxed on that occasion about the situation, having seen Luke moving both his arms and legs. Luke was also sharing the odd joke with the paramedics. As so often is the case, one of the first questions a medic will ask is how old the boy is and we received on this occasion the usual response, "wow, he's a big lad!" The paramedics struggled to lift him but eventually we made it to hospital, x-rays were taken and Luke was given the all clear on this occasion and as I recall, was playing a week later.

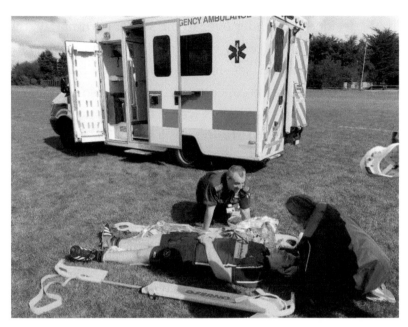

This was the scene a year before! Some might have called it a day after this scare but as it turned out, he was fine and was playing a week later! You can see the paramedic sharing a joke with Luke, most likely about how they were going to lift him. The other interesting thing about this photo, is that Luke is wearing the boots Mako Vunipola wore representing England in the 2015 World Cup! I was in Kapeli Pifeliti's room in my boarding house. He is Mako Vunipola's cousin and had a range of boots lined up on his shelf. I saw he had some 21mm studs in a pair and I asked him how I could get hold of some for Luke as the winter was setting in and they struck me as perfect for the front row. KP said "you can take those". I thought he meant the studs as I knew they were Mako's boots, so I said I'd return with a stud key. KP was quick to say "No, just take the boots!" What a lovely gesture and of course Luke was SO excited!

I now decided to wander over to the scene. Fortunately, the doctor's English was pretty good and while he was calm and professional, I could see he was concerned, but he was expertly concealing his concern from Luke. I also recognised in Luke that all was not in fact well. There was no sharing of japes and banter with the medical staff this time. I was reassured to see some movement in his arms and legs though Luke was complaining of pain in his right arm and was describing a bizarre kind of delay in its movement. Evidently there had been some kind of neurological damage and I think this was the origin of the doctor's concern. Once again, I was watching Luke having a neck brace fitted and being strapped to a spinal board. At the time, Luke was a 6'3", 97 kg 15-year-old boy and it was no small feat lifting him and carrying him to the far side of the field. He lay on the ground for some time, passers-by issuing brief messages of goodwill in both languages and offers of coats and warm tops to keep him warm were made. It was at this time that I was delighted to see Jacob, Angus and Pitu return from hospital. Jacob was on his feet though relying heavily on the two crutches that he had been given and Angus reported to me that Jacob had not sustained a serious injury. He was in fact reassessed on his return to the UK to find that in reality, he had ruptured his ACL and partially torn his MCL, surgery would be required and Jacob ended up spending a long, long time in rehab. That said, we knew nothing about that at the time and it was really good to see him back.

We decided to move Luke to the club's office in anticipation of the ambulance's arrival in the car park. I remember this looking quite strange as Luke was lifted onto the reception desk. This was a small office with a couple of tables behind the reception with computer screens, filed papers, books and a wide range of rugby memorabilia hanging on the walls. A couple of officials sat at these desks continuing their work, occasionally raising their eyes at Luke and me to issue a reassuring look. Luke was lying lengthways along the reception desk, barely fitting, his size 13 boots poking up into the room. Unfortunately, strapped in as he was, Luke could see nothing but a few square feet of ceiling right above his face. The ambulance took some time to arrive, certainly enough time for me to start getting a little prickly about it. I knew absolutely nothing about the medical system in Argentina. I had no idea what to expect, I was unaware of the standards that were in place and was completely in the dark as to the level of medical care that Luke would receive. My mind was in overdrive playing out a vast range of scenarios. I was continually trying to reassure Luke, to relax him and above all, trying not to communicate my inner anxiety in any way.

Eventually, the ambulance arrived and in walked the paramedics. I recall being in some way reassured that they were wearing a uniform. We went through the usual process of them staring at Luke in disbelief, the proverbial head scratching and the double-checking that everyone had understood correctly that he was only 15! A plan was quickly discussed for moving him from the reception desk to the ambulance or at least I think that is what was talked about as it was all in Spanish and once again, Luke and I were completely in the dark. I do remember there seemed not to be the levels of urgency that I might have hoped to have seen. I was invited to sit in the back of the ambulance with Luke and by now, I was running out of reassuring things to say to him. The first 200m of our journey was along the uneven gravelly track leaving the club. My levels of anxiety rose dramatically as I could see Luke being shaken from side to side by the ambulance shuddering along. With the immobilisation collar on, no doubt there was no real risk to Luke, but it was a worrying spectacle and not at all easy to watch. After what seemed like ages we finally moved onto tarmac and we experienced a smooth ride all the way to the hospital. I had been told that we were going to a place called the Clinica Francesa, which meant the French Clinic. Being half French and having plenty of family in France, I found this to be a good omen and I clung to that for reassurance. On arrival, Luke was wheeled down a corridor and into a triage room. The place seemed small and basic but in good shape. At this stage I was still reasonably calm, clinging to the possibility that this was a repeat of the previous year when an x-ray had shown nothing. We waited.

Pitu arrived which was comforting as communication was absolutely impossible. Tano, the manager of the U17 Los

Tordos team we had played against, turned up too. I recognised him from the billeting process and he had also been prowling the touchline with his own clipboard and stopwatch during the games. He spoke no English but somehow he managed to communicate his offer of help, asking me if I wanted anything: water, food, anything. Though communication with Tano was difficult, what became abundantly clear from the start was that this was a kind and concerned man who was offering unconditional support. Juan, Tomi's father, with whom Luke had stayed the night the eve of the game also arrived and offered his support. Both Juan and Tano had sons in the LTRC team and were clearly empathising with this worried English dad, 11,000 km from home. Juan, who was the former president of LTRC, spoke pretty good English and that was a real boost. Luke was taken for his x-ray. We waited.

My expectations of the quality of medical provision available in Argentina, driven entirely by ignorance, were not high but so far I was pretty pleased. Like any Accident & Emergency room in the world, strangers sat side-by-side, some waiting patiently and some less patiently. The usual routines were being observed; being moved from one room to another, and back, alongside explanations in Spanish about what was happening, all translated by Pitu. Luke had been seen quite quickly but was gone some time, as alongside an x-ray, he was also given a CAT scan. I kept repeating those words to myself: "this is all just a precaution".

After a long wait, we were invited into a new area and Luke was parked up against the wall at the far end of this long room. Pitu and I were ushered to the other end of the room by the doctor who had first welcomed us. He was a youngish man in his late 20s I would think, whose right hand had been significantly affected by some kind of deficiency, being much smaller than one would expect and I'm quite sure it was not fully functioning. It was a side issue entirely but I had noticed it from the start. He was a short man with a very kind but professional outlook. I could tell from his body language and facial expressions that Luke was not entirely out of the woods. Naturally I was very anxious. The three of us crowded around a computer screen as the doctor began to explain the details of the test results. Pitu would translate into English for me. My knowledge of Spanish was practically zero, however being half French and having taught French for over 20 years, it's incredible how much you can pick up in terms of the gist of what is being said. Once again I noted the facial expression of the doctor and words like "fractura" were not difficult to decipher. It was also painfully obvious, that Pitu was emotionally moved as the doctor delivered his news. His eyes were filling with tears and his voice shaking as he began to transfer the doctor's meaning into English for me. Despite having only known Pitu approximately a week, we had eaten and drunk together three times a day, socialising and bonding, through common ground like being family men and the inescapable strength of the bond between rugby players, no matter where in the world you may have played the game.

Pitu, showing great strength but whilst being visibly upset, passed on the details. I mentally braced myself. The doctor, during his explanations, had been pointing at the screen of his computer with a pencil. Pitu and I had been nodding but essentially saw nothing with our untrained eyes. However, the explanation left no room for ambiguity.

The human spine is made up of four main sections. The Cervical section, at the top of the spine is made up of eight vertebrae starting with the C1 at the very top, down to the C8 below which appears the Thorasic section, T1-T12. The Lumbar section runs down to the pelvis and contains five vertebrae, L1-L5 before the five vertebrae of the Sacrum takeover, S1-S5. The whole structure is completed with the coccyx at the very end.

Pitu delivered his news. Luke had a burst fracture of the C4 and significant lesions to the spinal-cord which explained his neurological pains and reactions in his right arm. Concerned that Luke could potentially hear all this, I encouraged the doctor and Pitu to move the conversation into the corridor. The doctor went on to explain that Luke was in urgent need of major surgery. I must say, that I didn't take this news as a shock. There had been enough clues in terms of the doctor's body language and eye contact. A number of thoughts ran through my mind. The most significant of these anxieties in the first instance was how Luke and I were going to manage this scenario speaking no Spanish and having no knowledge of the Argentinian medical system. In addition, we would have to attempt all this without the help of Pitu, who was moving on to Rosario with the tour party at 7am the following morning. A massive sinking feeling came over me. However, I had to focus on the next job and steel myself mentally and physically to communicate all this to Luke.

As I approached Luke I could see tears rolling down his face. He was of course still strapped into the spinal board and his head completely immobile. Staring straight upwards he had been unable to wipe his tears and his cheeks were sodden. As I arrived and stood next to him he spoke first. "I heard all that!" I wiped his tears and first apologised for the manner in which he had received this news. He calmed down and I reassured him that he could be fixed and that being able to move his arms and legs was a good sign. The diagnosis had been very clear and they knew exactly what to do to make him better. I explained that the next day he would be having an MRI scan to confirm the diagnosis and to identify the extent of any soft tissue damage. Luke was still 15 at the time. Despite his tears, which had subsided once I had returned to his side, I remember being struck by how calm he was. There was no sense of panic nor self-pity. It was only the first of two occasions during the whole episode that he cried. He demonstrated maturity beyond his years. Possibly, he may not have understood the gravity and precarious nature of his injury. I, on the other hand, was almost permanently on the brink of tears for about a week.

After delivering the news to Luke and ensuring he was as comfortable as was possible and warm, I walked out into the corridor to find Juan and Tano, who were receiving the news from Pitu. I stood near them and leant back against the wall of the corridor. While speaking with Luke my entire body was aching to cry, but I knew I had to present a solid appearance of support for him. Now, out of sight, I began sobbing. I don't recall now which of the two approached me, but either Tano or Juan came over and simply placed his hand on my shoulder; a simple gesture of empathy and support, but it seemed a symbolic one as the meaning was clear......*we are here for you.*

Once I had regathered my senses and dried my eyes, Juan communicated in more detail (and in English) what I had felt when he or indeed Tano had grasped my shoulder. They and others from Los Tordos Rugby Club would support us in any way necessary, for as long as necessary until Luke and I were safely on our way home. I could tell instantly by the manner in which this message was delivered, that the offer this man was making was not being made lightly, nor would it be taken lightly. I felt a huge sense of commitment and genuine assurance.

Luke and I were taken to a two-man room on the third floor with ensuite shower and toilet. It was pretty basic, but I remember being reassured that he was not sharing. Watching him being removed from his trolley and the spinal board was extremely frightening. A couple of the larger hospital porters had been recruited to the task of shifting this near deadweight of 97 kg onto the bed. Remembering the doctor's comments about how delicate and potentially unstable the injured area of his vertebrae was, the whole process was incredibly worrisome. However, these two large chaps expertly but pretty unceremoniously slipped Luke across onto his bed. The top half of the bed was elevated to 45° and we were told that until he had his surgery, this was the highest he could raise his head. The collar that had been placed on his neck by Peco, the club doctor, was still in place, indeed he was still in his match kit. Eventually, Luke needed to go to the toilet and I had the first of many, many difficult exchanges with the staff on the corridor.

Communication problems are rarely completely unsolvable. I became fairly reliant on Google translate and its various different features. I later also downloaded a Spanish verb app onto my phone which I found very useful. Google translate has a feature where you can speak your language into your phone, press a button and the other language, spoken by a pleasant sounding lady who no doubt doesn't exist, comes out! As the days passed, I became wary that the longer the sentence you put to Google translate, the more confused it gets and there were certainly a few accidental but humorous translations along the way. For stand-alone bits of vocabulary, it was super helpful. So our first attempt was to explain that this 15-year-old needed to go to the toilet and was not able to raise himself out of his bed to shuffle to the ensuite. What to do? After what must have been four or five attempts to communicate the situation, involving a range of mimes and other movements, eventually the *peso* dropped and the nurse disappeared into the store cupboard. He returned with a plastic receptacle which I thought resembled something not unlike a mini Roman amphora. I'd never seen such a vessel let alone used one so I launched an even more challenging communication task by seeking advice on how to use it. The nurse's demonstrations were pretty clear and I passed the information on to Luke.

Like any 15-year-old boy, Luke was not overly impressed at the prospect of having to urinate while lying in his bed and even worse, with his father looking on. Naturally he put it off for as long as possible but eventually, he had to give it a go. I assisted him as much as he would let me before walking around the corner of the ensuite to offer him some privacy. Later he told me his main concern was that this receptacle, which was designed to hold a litre of urine, would overflow. Indeed, he had cause to be concerned. I was utterly astonished to see that he had nearly filled this pot. A handy gauge on the side allowed me to measure this first effort: 950 millilitres!

Eventually, I felt strong enough to make the phone call to my wife Celeste, Luke's mother. I knew she had been at a music festival that weekend and had no doubt had a great time. Initially there was a short exchange about how she had enjoyed the weekend, but it was not long before I was delivering the news. I painted as positive a picture as was humanly and linguistically possible! I could not hide the facts, however, but like my exchanges with Luke, I emphasised the positives such as him being able to move his arms and legs and that he was not in any great pain. There was a clear path ahead involving a flight home and surgery in the UK after which he would likely make a full recovery. There was no disguising Celeste's anxiety at the other end of the line, but I felt at the time I had done a good job minimising her upset and worry. Basically, I felt the call had gone as well as it could. I promised to keep in touch and keep Celeste updated and I urged her not to worry unduly. I was probably wasting my breath with that one! Luke's older brother Matthew was at home dealing with the fact that he had come up short of his university offer at Durham by one mark. So Celeste was managing his disappointment and university application in the UK while I was managing Luke's unfolding story in Argentina. Fortunately for Matthew, a re-mark of one of his English papers yielded an 11 mark upgrade; totally unprecedented in my experience! So, after a little to-ing and fro-ing with the university, he ended up securing his place at Durham; a happy ending for one son.

Luke was reasonably comfortable, lying as he was at a 45° angle and not short of pain relief! The evening meal was our first experience of the food. It was pretty satisfactory and certainly better than one would have received at home. The tour party and staff were spending their last night at the hotel and once I had reassured Luke that he would be fine, well looked after by staff and confirmed his phone was charged and had my number I eventually and reluctantly returned to the hotel. Despite it now being quite late, Juan had arranged for another parent from Los Tordos and his wife to pick me up from the clinic and return me to downtown Mendoza. There was no question of me trying to sort out a taxi and make my own way! At the hotel, I was given yet another phone number and told by this nice couple not to hesitate if I needed anything…. anything at all. The players had long since been sent to bed and I found Jon, Angus, Joe and Pitu, sat at a table at the bar, quietly nursing their beers. I updated them on Luke's situation though Pitu had already filled the chaps in on his return from hospital. I was reassured and pleased to hear that Angus had taken on the responsibility of communicating with the school's insurance company. Essentially, it was made clear to me that I need focus only on Luke and that Angus would deal with the insurance side of things, ably supported by Pitu, who would be the key to liaising with the company's Buenos Aires office. I didn't fancy a drink as I recall but I do remember feeling as relaxed as I had been all day. I even managed to get through the conversation without crying. As we turned in for the night, I said my goodbyes to all but my roommate Joe as the tour party was leaving for Rosario at 7am the next morning. As I lay in bed, I tried hard but failed not to play out a range of worst-case scenarios in my head. What if the insurance would not pay for the surgery? What if Luke in some way slips or otherwise damages himself between now and the surgery, during the flight perhaps? What about turbulence? What if there's a problem during the surgery? Eventually I dropped off and slept soundly until I was woken by Joe as he was taking a quick shower and packing the last of his effects before disappearing off for some breakfast and onto the coach. We had a quick chat as he packed his bags and Joe offered a few last words of support and encouragement before heading off into the corridor, closing the door behind him. At that moment I felt very alone.

It was a reality check. I had known for some time that the tour, my colleagues and Pitu would be leaving, but seeing Joe walking out into the hotel corridor and closing the door behind him was a moment of brutal clarity. I'm usually comfortable in my own company perhaps having grown up as an only child, but now the stark reality of facing this scenario by myself made me physically feel ill. I lay in bed with my heart racing, thumping in fact, and my temperature seemed to rise to what felt like the mid 40 degrees as I began sweating profusely. My thoughts turned to how lonely Luke might also feel. He had not even had the benefit of a warm goodbye from his roommate. He was in an awful situation, alone in his room with nobody but the non-English-speaking staff for company and nothing to look at but a bland patch of ceiling. I decided to get up, shower and seize the day; the sooner I got back to the clinic, the better.

The breakfast room at the hotel, which doubled as the bar area outside of mealtimes, was very nicely decorated with a modern feel. It was a beautiful buffet breakfast which I had tucked into with great enthusiasm the previous day. That morning, however, I had absolutely no appetite. I sipped my way through a coffee and ate a banana in slow time. I attempted to nibble away at a few carefully selected offerings but it was no good. I just wasn't hungry. I returned to my room to prepare for the day then set off with Juan, who had kindly agreed to pick me up from the hotel and take me back to the clinic. That Monday was a bank holiday and the streets were quiet.

The clinic seemed quiet too and clearly, only a skeleton staff remained to run the place. There was no office or admin staff at all, so there was no prospect of any progress in terms of information or movement regarding communication with the insurers. I spent a rather long, dull day in the room with Luke chatting away about this and that with long periods of silence. There was no Wi-Fi available and anybody with teenage children will recognise the catastrophic nature of the situation, in some respects far more serious than a fractured vertebra! I was still hugely concerned and anxious about

Luke's situation, but I do recall feeling that this was a nice opportunity to spend some time together albeit in the worst of situations. It was a selfish feeling.

Throughout the day, nurses would come and go, conducting various tests on Luke and delivering what seemed to be a cocktail of pain relief and other drugs. I confess I had absolutely no idea what was being injected into my son! Communication with the nurses was nigh on impossible though a degree of success was occasionally achieved with the help of my increasingly close friend, *Google translate*. Luke was taken at some point for his MRI scan but the day was uneventful in general. We were visited throughout the day by Tano and Juan at different points and they made me aware of the WhatsApp group, which they had set up in order to support Luke and me and ease communications between key players in the situation. Both Juan and Tano were on the group, along with Pitu, who was now in Rosario with the tour party, a chap called Cesar and a few other Los Tordos dignitaries. I had taken a photograph of Luke in his hospital bed that day. The WhatsApp group had been called "Luke in Mendoza" so I uploaded that image as the profile photo.

The day went very slowly, punctuated by visits to the coffee shop which I would come to know well and the occasional giant pee from Luke. It was my job to fetch the receptacle, walk around the corner out of sight, wait, retrieve the receptacle and carefully empty it into the ensuite toilet and give it a rinse. To this day I don't know what that contraption is called, in either language, but the two of us saw plenty of action for a few days. Indeed, when Juan was kind enough to buy me a sketch pad and pencil on one occasion when he had asked me if there was anything I wanted, when deciding what to draw, this 'pee pot' was the first thing that came to mind. Although I had plenty of time on my hands, it was the only drawing I did and it turned out quite well. Tano had also asked me if there was anything I needed and I had asked for baby wipes as frankly, Luke was starting to smell, particularly his feet which were still in his rugby socks. When the wipes arrived, I quickly put them into action and I couldn't help thinking this was a flashback to simpler times when Luke was a baby. I recalled being able to wash him in the sink in our bathroom at home. No chance of that these days! I wiped his feet clean and encouraged him to have a good freshen up of the areas that he could reach. We both felt better about life.

Tano and Juan had not allowed me to pay for any coffees; "Out of the question!" The coffee shop was a typical chain style like in any hospital around the world. This one was called *Bonafide* which I gather is a famous chain in Argentina. The young ladies who worked there were very nice and supportive as I was slowly learning a few key words in Spanish. In fact, the following week Juan told me that one of these girls turned up to his office to interview for a vacancy at his work. He recognised her immediately from his visits to the hospital coffee shop with me. I've no idea if this was a significant factor or not but apparently, she got the job! The whole side of the coffee shop was a giant window looking across the busy main road opposite the hospital. On the other side a huge apartment block was under construction, with hundreds of workers diving in and out of rooms carrying out their various tasks; a bare concrete construction seven or eight stories high with steel bars poking up in all directions. Behind the construction site, Mendoza spread out and beyond; the magnificent sight of a snow-capped mountain range framed the whole picture. It was a great view in fairness with plenty to look at including a giant McDonald's advert. Later that day, Juan asked me, "What would make Luke happy?" and the first thing I could think of was McDonald's! Juan and I slipped off and ate at the McDonald's publicised on the giant poster opposite *Bonafide*. The power of advertising eh!? I was interested to read the menu. I thought McDonald's was the same wherever you went in the world, but I was ignorant of the fact that wherever you go they tweak the range on offer to suit the local palate and customs. Why wouldn't they? It was so obvious. The range of burgers here was huge and meat heavy! I enjoyed my meal and enjoyed chatting with Juan. He struck me as a really nice guy. He had spent most of his day off at the clinic supporting Luke and me and now was treating me to supper. We selected some food for Luke and drove back to the clinic. A simple offering of junk food was enough to bring a huge smile to Luke's face and I sat and watched him eat with great joy. All was not so bad. However, it was not all that easy for Luke to eat at a 45° angle, while not moving his head. In addition, the straw only just about reached his mouth without the rest of his Fanta pouring all over him. Despite the logistical challenges, he scoffed the lot with great glee!

Once again I left for the hotel, very reluctantly. I had enquired as to whether it was possible for me to sleep at the clinic in the spare bed. I was told that the second bed would likely be used for another patient. Luke was clearly tired and I wasn't all that comfortable about leaving him. Once again I confirmed that he had my number, then left. Juan drove me back to the hotel and I sat in his car, weeping in the passenger seat most of the way. He parked up right in front of the hotel and we sat for a while. I pulled myself together, thanked him for his support and headed off to my room. Juan made sure I was in no rush and spoke with me until I felt better. That night my hotel room felt very empty and I cried myself to sleep considering the worst-case scenario. What if Luke is paralysed during surgery? My mind then moved onto other things: Luke will never play rugby again, a game that had been so good to me and brought me so many positive things in my life. It would have been an important year for Luke and his progression. The previous year, he had been on the cusp of an invitation on to the Saracens Junior Academy (EPDG), but had fallen short. The coming season therefore would have been a key one in order to work hard and make a case for selection. I knew of course that all that was now up in smoke. The reality was that he had been very lucky not to be paralysed in the first place and this was far more important than Luke's ambitions to push his rugby as far as it could go.

Eventually I fell asleep only to be woken at 01.45 in the morning. My phone was ringing and picking it up I could see not only the time but Luke's name on the screen. He was in tears at the other end of the line barely able to speak. "I can't sleep" I detected through the sobs. "They keep coming in and doing things to me", "they keep switching the light on", "I can't sleep". I was furious with myself for leaving him and told him very simply, "I'm coming right over…don't worry." I immediately packed in haste and went downstairs to the hotel reception. I made my explanations to the 24-hour receptionist who had perhaps hoped for a bit of quiet rest at that time of the night. I asked him to order me a taxi and checked out of the hotel remembering to collect my receipt (I didn't dare invite accounts to kick up a fuss on my return) as Jon had very sensibly and kindly thought to leave me with one of the two tour credit cards for emergencies. On arrival at the hospital I walked in, got the lift up to the third floor and walked along the corridor and into Luke's room. I found an exhausted son, in tears with frustration. He was pleased and relieved to see me and after some reassuring words I curled up, fully clothed on the other bed and tried to sleep. I couldn't.

I had stood by his bed for a while and had apologised for leaving him yet as I lay on my bed, staring across the room at him, I couldn't shake off an overwhelming feeling of guilt. Why on earth had I made the decision to leave him and go back to the hotel? What must have been going through his mind as he saw me walk away that night? I was so angry with myself. If only I had taken a short while to make a more measured decision, surely I would have seen that the best course of action would have been to make a fuss at the hospital and refuse to leave my son. Maybe my brain was sufficiently scrambled by the stressful situation in which we found ourselves, that I was incapable of thinking more clearly. It's a poor excuse! Maybe there was an element of (subconscious) selfishness in the decision. In any case, it was doubly frustrating that I was now lying on the bed that we had been told might be needed for another patient; the very reason I went back to the hotel. It reminded me of a time I gave Luke the lid of a can of tuna that I had just removed with instructions to place it in the bin in the next room when he was only four years old. All he had to do was walk over with the lid between his thumb and forefinger, lift the lid of the bin and drop it inside. Yes, the lid was sharp but I considered it such a simple task that my four-year-old son could complete it with great ease. The next thing I knew, Luke was shrieking at the top of his voice having badly cut his finger on the lid of this can of tuna. The whole thing was so avoidable and I remember calling myself an idiot over and over again. So once again I found myself questioning whether I was a rubbish father... or an idiot... or both!

A Fresh Start

Tuesday was a bright sunny day and had a different feel to it entirely from the word go. The sluggish feel of the previous day, a bank holiday, was gone and there was a busy and purposeful feel to the place where people were scuttling in all directions carrying out their tasks. A smartly dressed, smiley lady, small in stature, but clearly influential, strolled into the room and introduced herself. She momentarily put down her clipboard and phone to shake hands and walked over to speak with Luke. Her name was Paula and she introduced herself as the person in charge of patient liaison. Her English, I was relieved to hear, was excellent. She explained to us that due to the MRI scan results, it was impossible for Luke to travel home before any surgery could take place and that this was a priority now. I had had a sixth sense that news of this nature was on its way. I was increasingly reassured about the quality of medical cover available and was increasingly comfortable now with the concept of Luke having surgery in this place rather than in the UK. She had good news too! We would be moving to a nicer "VIP" room on the *segundo piso* - the second floor - which sounded great and I was officially allowed to 'move in'.

This room was great with two comfortable looking beds, a TV, a super comfortable easy chair which I was looking forward to sinking into and a much nicer ensuite bathroom. I enquired about Wi-Fi. She reluctantly, but very kindly, gave us the Wi-Fi code for the *segundo piso.* "Don't tell anyone I gave you this!" What a game changer for Luke and his morale with the world of Netflix and social media now at his fingertips. I must confess, I too was very pleased. Luke was able to communicate with the outside world and some of his buddies who had continued on the tour. It was much easier for me also to make full use of the WhatsApp group. How ever did we manage before Wi-Fi? I guess life was a lot simpler. Paula was clearly the woman who got things done! I had mentioned that the end of the bed was not allowing Luke to straighten his legs. The poor chap was uncomfortable enough as it was. She acted quickly and before not too long a maintenance man was up in the room simply screwing the end of his bed off - job done!

A very tall, smartly dressed man with white hair was next to knock on the door and wander in. He introduced himself as Pancho, a nickname I'm led to believe meaning hotdog, or at least I think that's what I understood! He was a quietly spoken chap whose English was excellent. He was an economist, finance man, and had been appointed by the Los Tordos RC group to deal with the hospital admin staff and put pressure on them to communicate with the insurers with the sole purpose to push forward Luke's surgery as soon as possible. One message that had come clear from Paula was that the clinic would not operate on Luke until the insurers had guaranteed payment. The norm was to have the procedure, pay up front and claim back off the insurance. I had been quoted 500,000 Argentinian pesos which, thanks to my new Internet connection, was calculated at about US$15,000. Paying up front was not going to happen!! It was good to meet Pancho and Luke and I were moved to see yet another element in place set up by Los Tordos with a view to supporting and helping us in this near impossible situation in which we found ourselves. It would take some time but eventually Pancho's efforts bore fruit. I was getting regular updates on the WhatsApp group and Pitu was also letting Luke and I know how the tour was getting on. What a difference a day makes. I felt reassured, well supported and for the first time in a while quite optimistic. Every effort was being made on our behalf and I was able to focus fully on simply being there for Luke. I later found out that one of the co-owners of the clinic was a member of LTRC. That may have explained our move to a VIP room!

Juan took me out for lunch. I was excited to get out of the hospital and reassured that Luke was happy with his phone and his Wi-Fi! We sat down in a bustling popular restaurant with fabulous decor. The atmosphere in there was fantastic and a great relief from the monotony of the inside of a hospital room. Juan helped me decipher the menu and I ordered the *Ojo de bife*. It was a fantastic juicy ribeye steak cooked to perfection, with hand cut chips served on a wooden board with some sort of garlicky shallot sauce. It was just spectacular. Juan ordered a bottle of Malbec or was it a local Cabernet Sauvignon? I don't recall. What I can say with rock solid certainty is that it was a lovely drop and I sat, most content, and as relaxed as I had been for some time. Our conversation was relatively easy. Juan was an interesting character. He too was a finance man, a former president of LTRC and was currently sitting on the committee responsible for the planning of the upcoming international rugby match taking place that weekend between Argentina and South Africa in Mendoza. I remember thinking how interesting that sounded. Juan told me that it may be possible that Luke would be visited by some Pumas, the name given to international rugby players representing Argentina. He suggested I didn't tell Luke just in case it didn't come off, but he was hopeful. I was pretty excited myself.

Back at the hospital I resisted the temptation to explain in detail to Luke how splendid my lunch had been. He was pretty relaxed and I sank into my fabulous easy chair for some post lunch serious sitting down. One of the nurses on this corridor was a charming young lady called Antonella. She had clearly taken a liking to Luke and I think it was mutual. She made a big fuss of him whenever she came into the room and a couple of days later when she was back on duty I noticed that she had had her hair done. I might have been imagining it but I thought she was keen on Luke. She was a little surprised and perhaps disappointed to hear that he was only 15. That said she was very kind and affectionate with Luke all the same.

All day, I had felt the constant presence of the Los Tordos guys. Juan had taken me for lunch but throughout the day we had new friends either visiting, taking me for coffee or simply hanging around in the corridor waiting to offer support or translate something if we needed it. Tano, the U17 team manager didn't speak a word of English but we managed all the same with our respective Google translate apps. It was possible to conduct entire conversations using this extraordinary technology. It seemed like only a matter of time before our two phones would simply begin speaking to each other without any input from ourselves. That would have been weird! Tano was an architect by trade and his son had been in the team that had played against us. One of our other visitors that day was a man called Gonzalo with his son of the same name. Gonzalo Jr was the captain of the Los Tordos team and came carrying a gift for Luke. It was a LTRC shirt. The offering of a shirt is a traditional and typical gesture in the rugby playing community, but, on this occasion, the act seemed to carry more weight and meaning. Luke and I were both struck again by the unconditional nature of care and frankly love that we were receiving from near total strangers. It was the rugby family and its values at its very best!

Later in the afternoon, two young chaps came to visit Luke. They had both played in the game on Sunday. Luke and I were taken aback when one said, "I was the player involved in Luke's collision". He had come to visit Luke and check on his progress, but also to apologise. We were hugely touched that he had made the decision to visit Luke. Had he brought a buddy with him for moral support? Perhaps but I thought it displayed a good deal of courage to drop in on us that way and a huge amount of integrity and maturity. Luke and I were very quick to make it clear to him that there was no need for an apology. This lad was able to describe in more detail how the injury had occurred. It was simply great to see all the support for Luke. The club has a Facebook page and an Instagram account and Luke's story had featured heavily on both platforms such that our story was reaching as far as other clubs in the area and beyond. Cesar told me that he had even been approached by a local radio station to do a feature on Luke. Word had clearly got out!

Late in the afternoon, the clinic's head surgeon spoke with us. His English was outstanding and we were relieved to hear that the insurance company had finally offered a guarantee of payment and that the surgery was scheduled for the next day, Wednesday. Pancho and Angus had clearly done a great job chasing up their respective ends and finally the UK office was talking to the Buenos Aires office which was talking to the clinic. I was incredibly relieved and optimistic. It had been terrible not knowing how things would pan out but for the first time, a clear path had been laid out in front of us. The surgeon explained what they would be trying to achieve and assured us that he would personally supervise the procedure. He went on to explain that Luke would need to take a shower before the surgery and staff from the hospital would help. He also said that the area around his neck would need to be thoroughly cleaned and that he would return before the operation to conduct that tricky exercise personally. It would require the very careful removal of the collar. The surgery was scheduled for 3pm Wednesday afternoon. I was straight on the WhatsApp group to share this with the guys. I had also been in contact with Darron Moore, Luke's coach at Hertford Rugby Club and John McGurk, the father of one of Luke's teammates who was also at the club. I had received a number of very heart-warming messages of support from those two which I passed on to Luke. Obviously throughout all these different phases, I was keeping Celeste informed and thanks to Paula and the Wi-Fi, we were all able to chat via video call on a regular basis. We were all set to just get on with it now.

Throughout, Luke remained utterly calm, philosophical and attentive, listening carefully to the surgeons and doctors. During this period, Luke and I had several matter of fact discussions about walking away from the game or exploring ways in which he could remain involved in rugby without playing. I was so impressed with the wisdom and good sense my 15 year old son communicated to me during these conversations. In truth, we didn't have many such discussions. I found them way more difficult emotionally than he did, I think!

Surgery Day

Wednesday began like the other days with an early morning visit from nurses, various tests and the administering of drugs. Then the charming lady from the domestic team arrived with her offer of *cafe con facturas.* It was a very welcome breakfast snack of coffee and local pastries. My Spanish was coming along nicely! We could expect the surgery at 3pm. A message on the WhatsApp group told me that later in the morning Pancho would be dropping in on us and he was going to take me for lunch. For some reason however when it came to it, I couldn't muster any kind of appetite. I was anxious about the surgery and made a half-hearted attempt at eating a mixed salad made up of local produce, a few items of which to this day, I cannot identify. I did enjoy Pancho's company, however, and during lunch I was fascinated to see a couple in their 50s sat next to us with a pitcher of red wine on ice. Each to their own, I guess. Pancho had never seen such a thing either. When we returned to the hospital, I was informed via Pancho's translating skills, that the surgery would be pushed back to 6pm. Apparently, there had been some kind of horrific car accident and a range of emergency procedures had been launched with scheduled non-priority surgeries postponed. I wasn't overly upset and genuinely hoped that those affected by the crash would make it. All the same, there was a nagging concern in the back of my mind that the surgeons would be all the more tired before getting to Luke.

A number of the Los Tordos guys had said they would come along and support me while Luke was in surgery so I thought to communicate the new timings on the WhatsApp group. I guess things may not have gone all that well in the earlier surgeries as it was pushed back again to 9pm and once again I found myself telling the guys on the group chat. The afternoon became a very long and frustrating waiting game. Eventually, the head surgeon, who had spoken to us the day before, arrived with a team of nurses. It was shower time! For a day or so already, Luke had been given permission to get up from his bed and walk to the ensuite to go to the toilet which had been a great relief... no pun intended! The concern was that he may slip in the shower so he was supervised by a couple of male nurses on this occasion. He kept the collar on during the whole process and I remember feeling sorry for Luke as he is a private kind of lad and for a 15-year-old boy, the rather public nature of his shower would have been an uncomfortable situation for him. But as was the case for almost the whole of this story, he showed maturity beyond his years and the philosophical mindset to just get on with it.

With some careful and close supervision, Luke returned to his bed, which was moved away from the wall so that the surgeon could position himself behind Luke's head. I watched on anxiously as there was a tangible tension in the room giving away the very delicate nature of what needed to be done next. That the head surgeon at the hospital had set aside time to conduct this exercise personally spoke volumes and made me very nervous. The velcro on the collar was slowly and meticulously disconnected by a nurse as the surgeon held Luke's head gently but purposefully between his two hands. When the collar had been entirely removed, the total circumference of his neck was entirely wiped clean with special wipes. Great care was taken. The inside of the collar which had not been washed since that Sunday was also thoroughly cleaned. There were at least six staff members in the room and I could sense them all observing the surgeon with great respect and hanging on his every word, as he gave clear and measured instructions. It seemed such a simple exercise but the attention to detail, the levels of concern shown and the absolute lack of any sense of rush impressed me greatly. This was not an establishment prone to cutting corners, I sensed. I was more confident than ever that Luke's major surgery in Mendoza, Argentina, would be a success. Perhaps this was even a matter of national pride at play? The collar was replaced with as much care as it had been removed and with a few final words of encouragement, the surgeon left the room. I congratulated Luke on his courage and patience and we went back to our waiting. In truth I was in awe of how Luke was dealing with this situation.

I contacted Celeste for a quick chat and catch up as naturally I had been keeping her up-to-date during the day. She was at home, at Haileybury with Luke's older brother, Matthew. They were receiving support of their own from the College

Chaplain, Rev Chris Briggs. He had visited them a number of times at home and that day they went to our beautiful Chapel at the time of Luke's surgery in order to light a candle each, say a prayer and have a private moment of reflection. It was a tense and emotional moment as both Matthew and Celeste were moved to tears. Chris's eyes also filled with emotion. I had known Chris for many, many years and it was a typical gesture of kindness from one of the best people I know. Yes, to a certain extent he was doing his job, but with Chris you know it goes far beyond any contractual arrangement. He does these things because he's a good man, a caring man who goes the extra mile for his flock.

After another short delay, at around 9pm, a team of staff arrived in Luke's room to take him up to surgery. I had to watch once again with great angst as Luke was manhandled off his bed. The technique was pretty basic but effective. The four corners of his fitted sheet were lifted off the mattress, and the trolley wheeled adjacent to his bed. Two strong-looking porters then grabbed the two nearest corners of the bed sheet, now just sitting loosely on top of his mattress, with only Luke's mass pinning it down and in one firm and decisive action, they simply pulled the sheet and Luke with it, sideways off his mattress onto the trolley. It was just *all business* from the porters; unceremonious but efficient. I found those moments absolutely petrifying. My real worry was that he would end up slipping between the bed and the trolley and fall to the floor. I was glad not to have been alone.

Gonzalo had returned to see us in order to be with me when Luke went for his surgery. I was glad; to see Luke wheeled off around the corner and off to theatre was a supremely anxious moment. Without Gonzalo there I would have certainly sat and considered all the worst case scenarios possible. The guys had organised some form of rota so that at no point in the evening would I be by myself. Gonzalo was a really nice guy and had arrived carrying an iPad to lend to Luke while he was in hospital. It was yet another thoughtful gesture and Luke was delighted that he would be able to watch his Netflix on a bigger screen.

Juan also arrived and the three of us chatted for a while before Gonzalo gave me *un abrazo grande,* a big hug, some warm words of encouragement and left us to it. Paula popped into the room on her way home to say good night and good luck. She also had to tell Juan and I that Luke was receiving too many visitors and that we should respect the visiting regulations going forward. I guess she was only doing her job and I could tell her heart wasn't really in it. It seemed pretty obvious to everyone that she was wasting her breath and we would continue ignoring these rules. In all fairness, I had absolutely no clue what the rules were!

Before heading home, Paula suggested that Juan and I leave the building and go for a walk and that some fresh air would help. She confirmed that Luke would be gone some time, close to 4 hours in fact, and therefore we had plenty of time. I was reluctant at first as I wanted to be in the hospital in the event that something terrible might happen during the procedure. Juan pretty much insisted we go, suggesting we would just do one block. As soon as we walked out onto the pavement I did actually begin to feel better and less anxious. Despite the proximity of a large road, I breathed in a good lung-full of fresh air (or at least what I was telling myself was fresh air) and we set off to the right to do a clockwise circuit of the block. It was a beautiful clear night and the moon and stars were staggeringly vivid. Just below and to the right of the Moon I could see Mars. It was one of those periods when the Earth was particularly close to Mars and we could see it with the naked eye. It made me think of home as I had been observing it before setting off to South America. I quickly became glad of Paula's advice. Each time we reached a corner with a view to doing a right turn and making our way back to the hospital, Juan convinced me to do "one more block". This happened for a number of blocks and it turned into a really good walk, finally terminating at an inviting looking coffee shop. We were pretty much the only customers, late on a Wednesday night as it was. We were joined by the father of one of the doctors at the clinic, himself part of the Los Tordos Rugby Club extended family, a family I was beginning to feel very much a part of.

As a French teacher, I enjoyed the opportunity to learn a few words and phrases in Spanish and I felt I was making good progress in a language I'd never spoken before. We had a couple of smoothies (probably the healthiest thing I had consumed since leaving the UK) before returning to the clinic. I said goodbye to this lovely chap whose name sadly I don't recall. He was yet another genuine fellow who had given up part of an evening to put a metaphorical hand on my shoulder and offer warmth and comfort. I had never met this man before and never saw him after.

Not long after Juan and I returned to the room, we were joined by Tano and Cesar. Cesar had kindly offered to do our laundry the day before and was returning with our suitcases, full of beautifully folded clean clothes. Cesar was an architect like Tano. In fact, days later, Juan and I ended up at a supermarket that had been designed by Cesar. He was a very passionate man and totally *rugby* in his manner; by that I mean he was genuine, utterly loyal to his club, his teammates and the strong values of our sport. These were the very values that were generating such warmth of spirit amongst these rugby men to give up so much time to support a complete stranger and his son. Cesar was not one to veil his passion and he routinely communicated it on the group chat with messages of support in English. While these messages were not always grammatically tiptop, the emotions and strength of meaning were crystal clear.

We chatted and we chatted and we chatted. It was getting late and I urged the guys to go home, explaining that I would be fine. They told me that there was no way they would leave me alone until someone came in to say that Luke was okay. If it turned out to be bad news, I would not be facing it alone!

Eventually at half-past midnight, a member of the surgical team knocked on the door and walked in. The four of us leapt to our feet and waited to hear what news this chap had for us. He spoke in Spanish and Juan did the translating. Just listening to the surgeon's words and watching his gestures and body language, I got the sense that he was passing on good news. Juan was also smiling as he listened. The surgery had been a success! They were extremely pleased with the outcome. Luke would remain in intensive care for the rest of the night and probably into the morning as he recovered. We were all ecstatic and the four of us hugged, in tears of relief and joy in equal measure. I remember the guys congratulating me and before they left we took an obligatory 'thumbs up selfie' for the group chat but also for the guys to post on the Los Tordos Instagram and Facebook pages. So many people were following Luke's progress. "Get some sleep", "we'll see you tomorrow" I was told. I asked Juan to explain in Spanish to the staff on the corridor not to disturb me during the night as Luke was not there. It had been a long day and I was physically and mentally exhausted. I was feeling optimistic and was reassured that all had gone well. I laid my head on the pillow, closed my eyes and slept soundly for the first time in days.

Left to right: Jon, Angus, Joe and me ready for some zip-lining action!

Left to right: me, Tano, Juan and Cesar in the hospital room after a long night and news of the successful surgery.

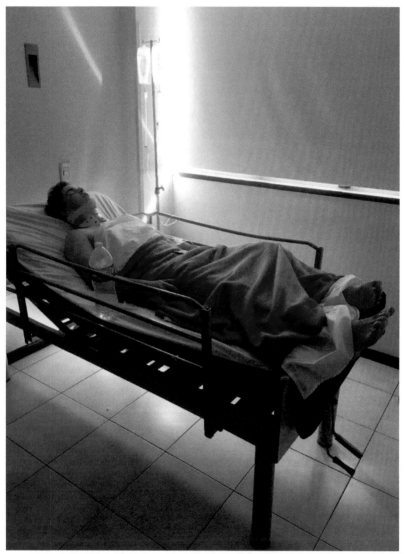

The profile picture for the *Luke in Mendoza* WhatsApp Group.

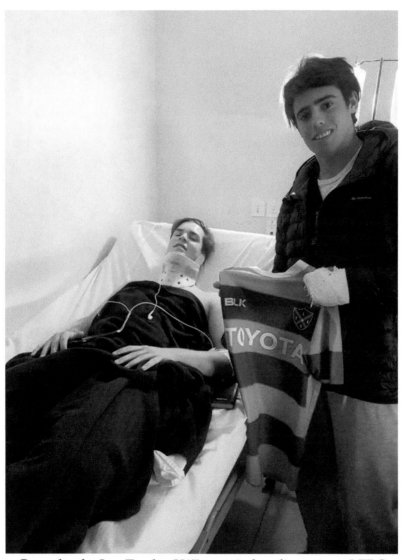

Gonzalo, the Los Tordos U17 captain handing over a LTRC
shirt to Luke when he visited.

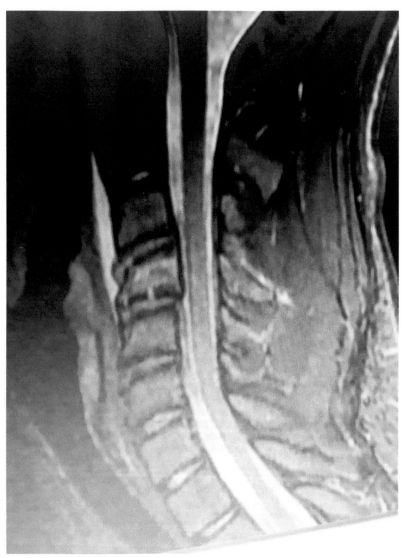

Luke's MRI scan, confirming the burst fracture and clearly showing how close he came to seriously damaging his spinal cord.

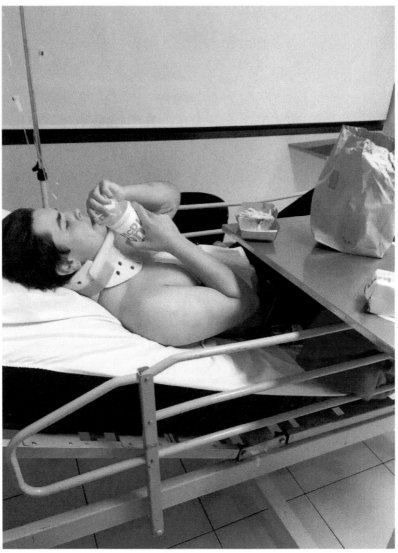

Luke was delighted with his McDonalds despite it proving
very difficult to consume.

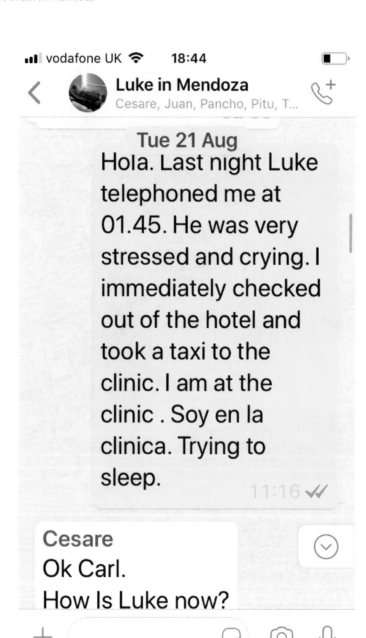

Tue 21 Aug

Hola. Last night Luke telephoned me at 01.45. He was very stressed and crying. I immediately checked out of the hotel and took a taxi to the clinic. I am at the clinic . Soy en la clinica. Trying to sleep.

11:16 ✓✓

Cesare
Ok Carl.
How Is Luke now?

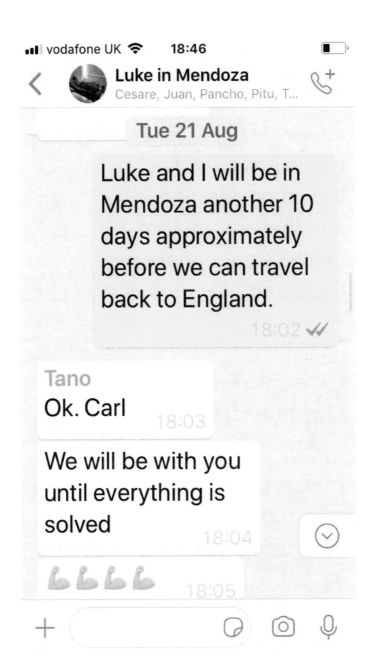

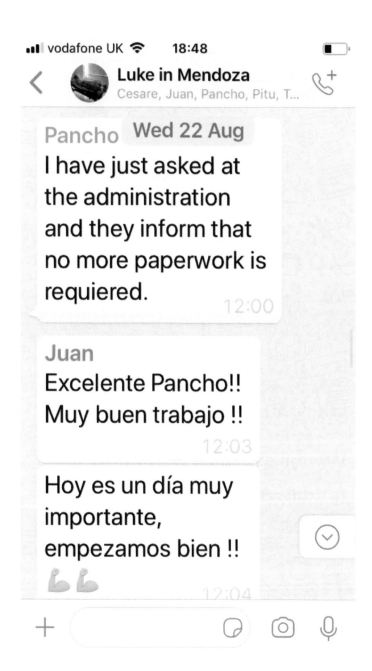

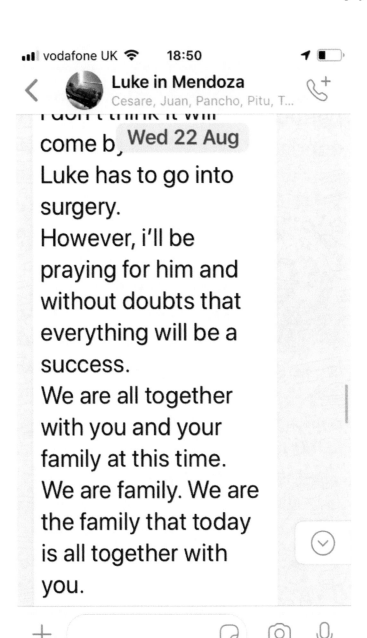

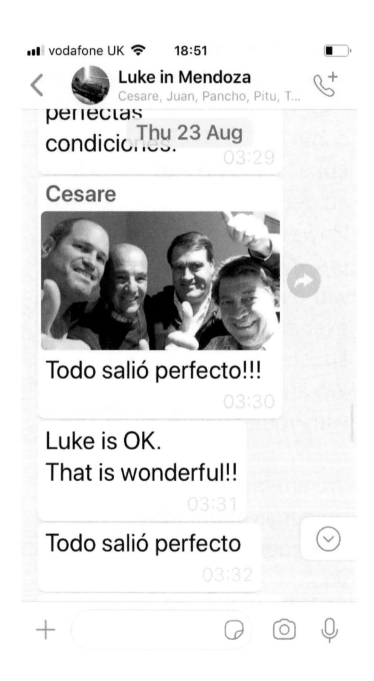

The Day After the Night Before

The next morning, it was a delight to have something of a lie-in and it really felt like having a day off. It had been such an intense few days that for a short while, glancing across the room at the empty bed actually felt like a relief. I had been told I couldn't visit Luke in intensive care until 10am and so I was determined to try to make the most of the slow start that morning. That said, it wasn't long before I really wanted to catch up with Luke and see how he was. I had a shower, got dressed and gulped down my *cafe con facturas*. I tried my luck at going into intensive care before 10 o'clock. There were a number of people waiting, but because I was now something of a resident at the hospital and Luke's situation was so well known, an exception was made. I was allowed in, told to wash my hands, then shown to Luke's bed. I hadn't really thought about what sight to expect. I really hadn't thought about it.

Luke was pretty much utterly out of it and covered in cables, stains and dressings. He was in a large cubicle about 5 m across and was lying on a special hospital bed, wired up in a range of locations to three or four different machines all seemingly beeping at different times, presumably for different reasons. His collar was back on, but underneath it I could see orange skin, stained from the iodine during the operation. There was also a small tube simply poking out of the side of his neck into a plastic bag hanging down by the side of the bed. It was a seriously odd look and I had no idea what it was there for. He was covered up to his belly by a sheet and there was an incredibly strong, almost overpowering smell of anaesthetic in the air. I was struck hard by how utterly helpless he appeared.

I stood for a while just staring at him. I'm not sure how long it was for but I reckon about 15 to 20 min. I took a photo to send to Celeste and eventually gave some thought to calling his name and seeing if he would wake. I was delighted to see some movement and we had a short exchange of words. "How are you?" I asked. "Tired" was his response. He was really dozy and clearly still on a significant amount of pain relief. After another short exchange he was able to communicate to me that I should go and fetch his phone, his charger and a pair of pants! I hadn't realised he was naked under the sheet and that was a situation he clearly wanted me to rectify as soon as possible. I realised I was serving little purpose as Luke drifted in and out of a deep sleep so I decided to leave and complete my errand! I left his phone and pants with the nurse and left them to get on with it.

A while later, back down in our room and after a long period of more serious sitting down, there was a knock at the door. It was Juan and a gentleman I had not seen before. I was pleased to see my new friend who introduced me to the stranger. This man was in his mid-50s and was wearing an Argentina Pumas puffer jacket. He was very smart and spoke good English; excellent in fact. He introduced himself as the Medical Director for the UAR, the Argentinian Rugby Union.

He said that he would like to go and meet with Luke and ask a few questions to see how he was. I thought this was a kind gesture from a man usually in charge of ensuring the Argentinian national rugby team were in tiptop condition. Before I took him to the ICU, I wanted to ask him a few questions. I was pretty direct. We discussed Luke's future in rugby and what his options were. During the previous days and long periods of waiting, Luke and I had discussed to a certain extent how he might continue to enjoy life involved in rugby if he were not able to return to playing. We had spoken about the possibility of coaching and even refereeing though I can tell you, Luke showed no real enthusiasm for that last suggestion. These had been sad discussions for me, but I was struck by how philosophically Luke had been able to approach the subject. So I asked this man, "If Luke's surgery is successful, and his period of rehab goes well, if he plays again, will the risk of him breaking his neck again, or worse, be greater because he's done it once before or the same?" He replied very calmly and genuinely, looking me straight in the eyes, "If the fusion is successful, the risk of him doing this again will be the same as any player taking the field." Those words rang in my head all day as I had simply assumed Luke would have to walk away from playing the game.

I took him to the ICU and it took him about eight seconds and a flash of his business card to convince the nurse who was guarding the door to allow him to enter and give him access to Luke. I was told to wait outside. Juan and I chatted and waited patiently. We had been used to that. A short while later, check-up complete, he came out of the ICU and we wandered back to the room. He reassured me that Luke was well and that all the signs suggested that the operation had been a success and while he was a little weak at the moment, Luke would make a full recovery. He did stress the fact that Luke's road to recovery would be a very long one and that patience should be at the forefront of everything we did. I thanked him and as he left, he placed his business card in my hand and said, "We are in Mendoza for the rest of the week. You have my number. If there is anything at all you need, please call me." I confess that once again I was moved to tears and sat by myself in the room with tears rolling down my cheeks. I was neither sad, upset nor anxious. I was simply blown away by the level of support that the both of us were receiving from total strangers. That, mixed with emotional exhaustion, was enough to set off the water works! It didn't last long and a little while later, Luke was brought down to our room and I had to suffer the sight of him being dragged across the mattress again. I really did hate it! It looked so dangerous.

Just a few hours before, under general anaesthetic, Luke's neck had been cut open at the front and just to the right of his Adam's apple. They had gone in sideways and began cutting out the damaged bone from his C4 vertebra. They cut downwards and lifted a cube shape of damaged bone which

I presume went straight in the bin. The next stage was to cut a similar size and shape bone graft from the right-hand side of his hip. I guess the thing would have looked not dissimilar to a nice big cube of feta cheese on a Greek salad. The square shaped hole in the vertebra was levered open and the feta cheese bone graft was dropped in. The levers were removed thus allowing the bone to clamp shut, holding the graft in place. Now a metal plate was placed on top with the ends overlapping the C3 and C5 vertebrae. This plate was then secured in place with four locking screws. I remember seeing an example of the metal plate and thinking it looked like something one might find on a shelf in Wickes. Anyhow, that's what was holding Luke's neck together!

Juan had mentioned to me a few days previously that it might be possible that some internationals from the Pumas squad, that were in town that week to play against South Africa that coming Saturday, might come to visit Luke. When we received the visit from the medical director I had assumed Juan had worked his magic and that was the visit he was talking about. He had urged me not to mention anything to Luke just in case it was not possible. Luke was slowly coming around and we were now able to converse pretty normally. He was tired but in good shape. By about mid-afternoon the day after his surgery, Luke was back in relatively good form again as we heard another knock at the door.

I opened the door to our hospital room to see three men, two of whom were immense in size, waiting in the corridor. All three were wearing Argentinian kit from top to toe and immediately I realised they were about to make Luke's day! As they walked in and appeared into view around the corner, Luke's face immediately lit up as he recognised what was happening. International scrum-half Tomas Cubelli, hooker Diego Fortuny and prop Juan Figallo had dropped in to cheer Luke up. It was amazing! Once again the folks in Argentina had astonished me with their willingness to support Luke and go out of their way to make the very best of a bad situation for us. The lads sat around Luke's bed and chatted for some time.

As we spoke, it became clear that two of them, Cubelli and Figallo had been to England during the 2015 Rugby World Cup and were familiar with Haileybury. How? Argentina had chosen our school as a base at which to prepare for two weeks during the campaign, staying at a local fancy hotel and using our facilities and pitches at which to train. I remember it being an exciting time for all rugby lovers in our area. The day they arrived, we had hosted the welcome ceremony during which each squad member was awarded his 2015 Rugby World Cup cap.

It was quite a coincidence. What was even more extraordinary was that the UAR Medical Director who had visited us earlier in the day had clearly returned to the squad hotel and hand-picked these three Pumas to come and visit this young English rugby player. Two of them were front row players like Luke (although he was expected to play second row on tour) and even more extraordinary, two of them had had exactly the same fusion surgery that Luke had experienced the night before. It was great watching these guys comparing stories with Luke and getting their phones out showing various MRI scans and x-rays. There was a real sense of empathy for my son and it was hugely encouraging in terms of the possibility of a return to playing rugby. Both Tomi Cubelli and Juan Figallo were sharing their experiences of the operation and the lengthy rehab process with us. They really emphasised the importance of being patient and simply allowing time to do its work in terms of fixing Luke.

They kindly brought Luke a Pumas cap and a hoodie which was also a very thoughtful gesture. Before they left we had a few handshakes and some photos and just as they were walking out of our door, Tomi Cubelli stopped and turned to face Luke asking him if he was on Instagram. Luke answered "yes" to which he replied "what's your Instagram, so we can keep in touch." I thought this was absolutely amazing and of course it goes without saying that Luke was completely made up! The visit of these three Pumas only added to Luke's fame in the hospital as the sight of these three internationals strolling down the hospital corridors drew a good deal of attention from the local staff.

Juan really came up trumps pulling this one off and Luke and I were now really looking forward to watching the

Pumas play against South Africa at the end of the week. I was only hoping that we would be doing it from a comfortable sofa somewhere rather than in our hospital room. I posted the photo on the WhatsApp group to the others and of course texted it to a few buddies in the UK.

I thanked Juan from the bottom of my heart and he was typically laid-back and cool about it. "Muy bien" he said, "Luke is happy." While it was a great event for Luke, I couldn't hold down my own personal excitement. It was turning out to be a really good day.

Post Operation Care

As promised, the surgeon, Mr Terraza dropped in to check on Luke. I thought it was remarkable that the surgeon himself would come and visit his patient the day after surgery to check on progress. He personally removed the dressings to check the stitching and clean the wounds. I was struck by the amazing attention to detail and the care that was being taken. Mr. Terraza was quite clearly a *smooth operator*...literally! He was a laid-back, relaxed kind of character but still supremely professional. His English was not too bad and he expressed himself slowly but with great clarity. He was always at pains to make sure that Luke and I understood every step of the procedure and indeed what would be happening next. I found out much later on, months later in fact, that Angus had done some research once back in the UK and found out that Mr. Terraza was one of the best in his field in South America.

He seemed very happy with the outcome and reassured both myself and Luke. He also explained the mystery tube coming out of Luke's neck. It had been placed there to allow excess fluids to drain out. One of his tasks that day was to pull the tube out. Watching on, it was one of the weirdest things I've seen. This very small plastic tube was pulled slowly and steadily out of my son's throat until the end popped out. I had been expecting blood and fluids to spurt out but thankfully there was nothing. The tube itself and its associated paraphernalia were discarded, the whole area carefully cleaned and new dressings applied.

The order from the surgeon was clear: "REST!" Thankfully, with Paula's gift of Wi-Fi and the iPad so thoughtfully brought over by Gonzalo, Luke's phone and a range of charging possibilities, no device would ever run out of battery. Luke settled with ease into a teenager's lifestyle of lying in bed watching stuff with his headphones on.

Luke would receive routine visits throughout the day and night by staff carrying out various tests and delivering pain relief via the various tubes and plastic bags of liquid suspended above his head. Communication with the nursing staff was really only possible with the help of Google translate. I really wanted to ensure I could understand on each occasion what was being done to Luke. On one occasion, we were woken in the night by the lights being switched on and a rather full chested nurse pushing a trolley of medication into the room. She blurted out a few lines in Spanish which meant absolutely nothing to Luke nor to me. I tried a few times to achieve some clarification with what little Spanish I had picked up over the last few days, but eventually resorted to using my phone and the Google app. Eventually I encouraged her to speak into my phone in order to translate her meaning. The Spanish word *control* has a meaning similar to *test* or *check* and as Google is not at its best translating longer phrases, a very humorous translation came out of my phone's speaker. While this big bosomed lady was hovering over Luke administering his medication, Google translate announced "Luke will have to control himself!" The poor lady was left scratching her head as I laughed out loud in the adjacent bed. Suffice it to say that I didn't attempt to explain my state of amusement!

On another occasion, in the middle of the night, once the tests had all been completed on Luke, a different nurse this time turned to me, walked across the room and began rolling my sleeve up to check my blood pressure. She was adamant and would not take *no* for an answer. Eventually and once again with the help of Google translate, I was able to explain that I was Luke's father and not just another patient!

Luke was making slow but significant progress. The most significant pain he was in was from the hip area where a large cube of bone had been removed. It was something the Pumas had mentioned during their visit and Luke could expect a good deal of pain from his hip for several days to come. Despite this pain he was now able to rise from his bed and hobble carefully to the toilet, dragging his drips along with him. Showering was still not really an option at this stage because of the wounds and dressings, so the wet wipes that Tano had brought along were still very much in good use.

We were still receiving regular visits from our new *amigos* from LTRC and we would have frequent coffees together at *bonafide*. I was becoming quite proficient at ordering two medium-size coffees in Spanish. We would sit sipping our coffees, chatting about Luke, rugby, Argentina and anything else to pass the time. It was actually a real joy glancing across at this incredible mountain range which was bathed in sunlight every day. The chaps across the road on the construction site seemed to be making good progress too!

One day, I was sat by the window drinking my coffee and chatting to Tano, when my phone rang. I heard an English voice at the other end of the line. He introduced himself as Dean Holder from the Injured Players Foundation (IPF) at the RFU. What became clear was that the UAR medical director who visited us the morning after Luke's surgery had not only returned to the hotel and arranged for three Pumas to visit. Evidently, he had also got on the phone to his counterpart at the RFU to explain that there was a 15-year-old English player, in a hospital in Mendoza having had surgery on a burst fracture of his C4. Dean was extremely sympathetic and spoke quietly and calmly on the phone. He was offering unequivocal support to do whatever was possible or necessary from their end. "If you need any assistance regarding insurance, hotels or flights, please don't hesitate to get in touch" was the message. Dean had caught me entirely by surprise and once again, I found the offer of care and unconditional support emotionally very touching. At times during our conversation I was moved to tears and was unable to maintain the conversation. I remember Dean assuming the periods of silence were due to a poor connection on our mobile phones. I had to explain that the phone was working perfectly well and that it was in fact me that was *cutting out*. I guess during long periods of waiting with nothing to do I was simply getting used to the situation and on the occasions – and there were many – when I was seeing outpourings of warmth, care and support for us, they were reminders of Luke's still very precarious situation but more importantly reminders of how good people can be. These moments were also frequent reminders of how I felt so sorry for Luke. The upcoming season was going to be an important season for him and his rugby progress. He had been looking forward to the prospect of a few games for Haileybury's 1st XV, more contributions to his club and county setups and continued attendance at the Saracens Player Development Group. The hope had been that the coming season would be another opportunity to push for a place in the Saracens Junior Academy. I remember showing Tano a photo of Luke from the one occasion the previous year when he had played for the Academy against Northampton Saints. I looked at Tano and said "His first game for Saracens... and his last." It was my own fault this time for saying such a thing but I had another weep. It was the only time I cried in the hospital room in front of Luke but he had his earphones in and hadn't heard the conversation and furthermore, his view was obscured by Gonzalo's iPad. *Muchas Gracias* Gonzalo!

Dean Holder went on to contact me several times during our time in Argentina with his offers of support, encouragement and kind words. We discussed a range of options for Luke to continue making contributions in rugby should he not be able to return to playing including coaching, refereeing and indeed fundraising. It was great knowing that he and his organisation would be waiting for us in the UK if we needed anything on our return.

Mr Terraza suggested to Paula that we might be discharged on Saturday morning so we just had a few more hospital meals to go! These meals were surprisingly good in fact and Luke and I would sit around a makeshift table that we had put together in order to make the best of the situation. I would do my best to prepare each meal for him in terms of removing various bits of cellophane, cutting up the meat and pouring drinks. I sort of look back on those meal times quite fondly as they were occasions when the iPad was switched off, the phone temporarily laid to rest and we sat together chatting and eating. Luke was able to sit upright in the comfy chair and had even been given permission to remove the collar from around his neck in order for him to eat before replacing it afterwards. There was also the convenience store, the *almacen* that I had discovered the night of the surgery during my walk under the stars with Juan. I popped in there a few times for treats! So we were making progress on many levels.

Luke was now routinely getting himself out of bed and walking to the ensuite bathroom to go to the toilet. It had occurred to me that if he could walk to the toilet then perhaps he could make it to the end of the corridor where the lift was, thereby opening the possibility of us popping up to *bonafide* for a change of scenery and a soft drink. I put the suggestion to Paula who had also given me her mobile number, something I'm quite sure she didn't do with every patient and thus I was easily able to communicate with her on WhatsApp. She said that she would check with the surgeon and get back to me. Not long afterwards, to my great delight, this was approved and we set about planning this great expedition! By now Luke was also off his drip and we gave him a good wash, pulled out some clean clothes that were folded neatly in our suitcase thanks to Cesar, and headed off down the corridor. The sight of Luke on his feet in the corridor was greeted with great pleasure by the hospital staff that we came across. Seemingly everybody in the hospital appeared to know about the two English residents on the second floor. In fact, I got the impression that by now, everybody in Mendoza knew about Luke. That was nonsense of course, but it felt like it.

Luke limped slowly but steadily down the corridor, still in significant pain with his hip but for the time being he was putting that to one side in order to accomplish the mission. I walked behind him and filmed him making his way down the corridor on his own two feet. I couldn't wait to post this on the group chat and I knew there were a few folks back in the UK that would appreciate seeing the site of Luke up on his feet. Paula had also decided to accompany us. Perhaps she didn't trust me when I promised we would take the lift not the stairs! We arrived at the coffee shop and the two *bonafide* girls that had been serving me for days seemed delighted to see Luke. I think we ordered a couple of Sprites and sat looking out of the window. I pointed out the giant McDonald's sign that had prompted me to go and fetch over a burger that second night. Once again the sun was out. Today the magnificent mountains looked more stunning than ever!

There was little else to do but stick to our regime of resting, recovering from surgery, eating our meals and routinely greeting the nurses as they came in and out with their tests and their drugs. Eventually, the concept of being discharged was discussed and once Mr Terraza had taken one final look at Luke, a decision was made to discharge him on Saturday morning, nearly a week after the injury. Juan and I had been discussing over the last few days, where Luke and I would stay after being discharged from hospital. There were really only two options. Firstly, we could stay in a hotel and claim back the cost from the insurance. That would surely be a simple process, yet Luke and I had absolutely no idea how long we would have to stay in Mendoza before flying home. We knew we had a follow-up appointment on Tuesday morning with our consultant surgeon but after that we had no clue. The hotel option was appealing however Juan had also offered for us to stay with him as had Cesar. Cesar had been unbelievably kind and attentive to us during this whole process and he seemed extremely keen for us to stay with him. For a short while, I sensed there may have been some competition between Juan and Cesar over who would get us to stay. I'm quite sure that this was a totally fictional invention of my imagination as at the time, while Luke's surgery had gone well, my mind was still a bit of a mess. The obvious choice for me, which was very much in Luke's best interest, was to take Juan up on his offer. Staying alone, just the two of us in a hotel in a town we didn't know, and not speaking Spanish would have been a hopeless exercise. Luke had already stayed with Juan and his son Tomi the night before the injury and therefore knew the home and the family already. While Tomi was going to school every day, at least Luke would have the opportunity after school to spend some time with another teenager (I think he'd had his fill of spending all day with his father) and I was certain that we would be well looked after. I know with all my heart that Cesar would have looked after us incredibly well too and I hope to this day, that he was not unduly saddened by our decision to stay with Juan.

Cesar had kindly done all our laundry and therefore our bags were packed and ready to go. We went to sleep on Friday night looking forward to a fresh start in the morning and a new phase in what was becoming quite an Argentinian adventure!

Argentina versus South Africa

We enjoyed the last of our hospital breakfasts, a couple more tests for good measure and we set about tidying the room in order to leave it in the best possible condition. It was the least we could do after all the care we had received. Through the WhatsApp group we had organised for Cesar to help with the discharge process as there would no doubt be various bits of paper work to fill out and potential linguistic entanglements with which he could assist. I also strongly believed that Cesar simply wanted to be there to enjoy the moment! And it was quite a moment! Luke and I stood by the admin desk, surrounded by all our suitcases, we signed off a few bits of paperwork, which I carefully placed in the file that I was keeping, and posed for the obligatory photo taken by Cesar. This was immediately posted on the group chat. I'm of the generation that can sometimes be overly negative and almost arrogantly dismissive of new technology and especially of social media. Sometimes in life, however, you simply have to take your hat off and this was one such occasion. The group chat on WhatsApp had been something of a lifeline and a genuine source of connection and encouragement to say nothing of the practical logistical value of communication that it offered. It was now also serving as a record of this whole story.

We set off in Cesar's car over to a rather splendid gated community where Juan lived. These gated communities could be found all around the outskirts of Mendoza with solid walls all around and only one way in and out, controlled by a security team. With swing gates controlling traffic passing in and out of these estates, containing several hundred homes, these were significant locations for only the most well-to-do and successful families. That was certainly my impression.

Juan's home was really lovely and decorated in what I assumed was a traditional Argentinian fashion. The ground floor was entirely tiled with exposed wooden beams in the ceiling. A huge open hearth was a focal point in the lounge and Juan had a large collection of books on show, along with family photos and other mementos from previous trips and expeditions. Tomi had kindly given up his room so that Luke could use it and he would sleep in his brother's room. We ended up staying almost a week with Juan and in a bizarre psychological twist that can only be explained by the fact that my brain had been completely scrambled and my focus was so completely on Luke that as I write this book, I have absolutely no recollection, absolutely zero, of where I was sleeping. I don't recall the simplest detail about my bedroom. Was I sleeping in a single bed or double? Was there one window or two? Presumably there was one window at least but what was the view? Whereabouts in the house was it? I can remember in great detail all the other places in the house. It's as if I did not sleep all week and simply remained upright in the lounge, kitchen or Luke's room. Very strange! Perhaps by the time I've finished this book it will all come back to me and I'll have to rewrite this paragraph!

Cesar left and Juan, Tomi, Luke and I had a spot of lunch: some pasta, salad and bread. It was a very exciting day that everyone had been looking forward to all week and probably longer than that! Argentina were playing South Africa at the main stadium in Mendoza. We had been told that the Pumas had an excellent record of success in their international games in Mendoza and so there was a good deal of optimism despite the Springboks being so strong. Juan as I mentioned earlier, had sat on the committee that had organised this international match alongside officials from local government, local security and the police and other senior gurus from various local clubs. I'm certain in my mind that Juan would have received a ticket or an invitation to watch the game live and that he had given this up in order to be with Luke and I watching it on TV in his home. Next to the generosity of spirit that he had already offered us, it seemed a small gesture but nonetheless, I was aware of its significance. Although I'm speculating, I'm sure Juan would have wanted to be at the game that he had played a part in organising. I do remember that Juan and some of the other chaps had been at a previous meeting with one of the surgeons during which, in Spanish obviously, Juan had been asking a range of questions about Luke's recovery and seeking advice about this and that which he would then pass on to me in English. While my Spanish is not great, my experience of French did help me greatly in gathering the gist and general thread of some conversations. During this meeting I got the sense that Juan had enquired as to how appropriate it would be for Luke and me to attend the match, only hours after our discharge. I understood that the consultant had plainly said no as being amongst the jostling crowds with the almost inevitable jumping up and down, cheering and celebrating would be in his view, an unnecessary risk. He was of course absolutely spot-on. So Luke and I would watch the game at home with Juan and his son Tomi.

It turned out to be a great game and the Pumas played out of their skin to record a famous and memorable victory over the Springboks. As strong as South Africa were, creative when in possession of the ball and physically challenging on the gain line, competing for every collision with huge intensity, the Pumas' defensive effort was quite simply up to the task and beyond. Their line speed was explosive and purposeful, taking collisions on their terms and making their tackles well beyond the gain line; they made life very difficult for the visitors. Single-minded in their defensive sets, the home side showed great determination to claim the ball back and made effective use of their turnovers. Argentina took their chances well developing a good lead which they defended successfully.

Things didn't start well for Los Pumas. In the 14th minute, Springbok captain Siya Kolisi slipped an attempted tackle from fly half Nicolas Sanchez 40 metres out and set off on a rampaging run to the line and thanks to some indecisive defending from the covering Argentinians, was able to power his way over the try line to open South Africa's account. That brought the score to 3-7 after an early Pumas penalty. The home side responded almost immediately. From a breakdown on halfway, a beautiful pass back inside from playmaker Sanchez, found his full-back, Emiliano Boffelli who stretched his legs showing great pace and making inroads deep into the Springbok half, before fixing a defender and passing it to the support runner who finally shipped it to young winger Bautista Delguy. Delguy screamed past the cover defender to score in the corner (10-7). Just moments later, from another very strong Argentinian set scrum which had 'gone up on 3' (nice work by Juan Figallo on the tighthead side) a number eight pick brought the Pumas well beyond the gain line. Argentina made good use of an overlap down the right-hand side and some less than convincing tackling allowed Delguy in for his second (17-7). Sanchez was next to score after a scrappy passage of play born largely from some terrific pressure at the base of an Argentinian scrum by Faf de Klerk. Sanchez's try was brought into question and scrutinised by the TMO as an unnecessary and overly flamboyant dive had almost led to him landing on the dead ball line. While Sanchez was in flight, his heart must have been in his mouth as there was little he could do about his trajectory once he'd taken off. But it was to be Sanchez's day as his try was awarded and he added a 47 m drop goal to his three conversions and one penalty. The half time score was an incredible 27-7 to the home side.

The second half began with the home side scoring within 6 minutes through left-wing Ramiro Moyano, who tore down the touchline to dot down in the corner and extend their lead to 32-7. All great sides recognise the importance of responding quickly and 2 min later Springbok winger Lionel Mapoe scored in the right corner after a magical cut-out pass from full-back Billy le Roux (32-14). Then in the 65th minute, Le Roux was instrumental again freeing his arms out of a tackle just short of the line and offloading to Mapoe who recorded his second try in the same corner. The try was unconverted and the final score was 31-19. The Springboks had the best of the second half but Argentina were stoical in their defence of the impressive lead they had built.

Luke and I, now fully fledged honorary Argentinians, were as delighted as the rest of the family! The game of course, was all the more exciting as we watched the players who had visited Luke just days before in hospital taking the field. Tomas Cubelli came on during the second half to replace scrum-half Gonzalo Bertranou, the former Los Tordos player. Juan Figallo put in a massive shift in the front row starting at tighthead. Neither of these two seemed unduly bothered by their surgery that had clearly been a success. We all hoped that would be the case for Luke.

We had been watching the game with a couple of beers and some Argentinian snacks and during halftime, simply by means of getting a conversation going, I asked Juan "what's the name of this stadium?" He had a little sparkle in his eyes and chuckled to himself before replying, "*Estadio Malvinas Argentinas*, The Argentinian Falkland Islands." I recognised that this was potentially a rather awkward moment though could tell from Juan's expression that there was no cause for concern so I replied, "Oh dear, we've managed to get this far without mentioning that!" The exchange was all very light-hearted despite the fact that Juan had served in the Argentinian army during the early 80s.

Luke spent the remainder of the afternoon resting as did I, perusing some of the books in the lounge punctuated with chitchat with Juan. I was beginning to turn my eye to the business of the new academic year and with the uncertainty of how long Luke and I would have to remain in Argentina, my concern turned to my boarding house. I run one of the seven boys' boarding houses at Haileybury, Lawrence House. There would be an induction day where new pupils in years 9, 10 and 12 arrive for their first day along with their parents. It's a crucial day for them but also for the house team and the concept of the housemaster not being there was one that concerned me deeply. Under normal circumstances, the Assistant Housemaster would happily and effectively take over the induction day process. However, on this occasion, my AHM had been appointed externally and himself would be new to the school; running my induction day would be a big ask!

In addition, there is always a team-meeting prior to the beginning of term run by the housemaster with his team of seven tutors. During this, a huge amount of information needs to be disseminated, and the important message of reinforcing the house culture and standards at the start of the new academic year. I was also likely to miss this meeting. I had received a couple of hugely supportive e-mails from school, most notably one from the Chairman of Governors and indeed one from The Master (Haileybury's Headmaster). In a reply to Martin Collier, The Master, I communicated my concerns and he responded with a very clear message. What was important was that I would support Luke and I was not to concern myself unduly with events at school. They would manage, come what may. I was hugely reassured and grateful for his support. I had been using Gonzalo's iPad for all of these communications with school so once again it had been a great help.

In the evening, Luke and I were introduced to a fabulous Argentinian tradition, the *asado*. Luke and I watched as Juan meticulously prepared a wood fire on top of the stone surface on his enormous, purpose-built outdoor barbecue. I was well aware by now of the expertise in Argentina in terms of preparing meat and indeed the respect they have for it. In the UK we are generally used to cooking on cheap barbecues from B&Q having popped down to the petrol station for a bag of overpriced charcoal, various fire lighting products and some cheap sausages and burgers from a local supermarket. If you're feeling in a fancy frame of mind, you might treat yourself to a prepacked selection of marinated drumsticks! I was therefore fascinated to observe this experience taking mental notes all along.

The *asado* is far more than a simple barbecue. It is a social event from start to finish. As Juan built up this wood fire, so bottles of wine were opened and served as guests arrived. Tano and his son were there and we met Michelle, Juan's partner for the first time. She was a lovely lady originally from Brazil who was incredibly caring and made a real fuss of Luke.

By now, with the help of various specific tools, Juan had moved the entire fire over into the corner of the barbecue area. I asked him why it was necessary to set up the fire in the middle and then move it to the corner when it seemed more sensible to simply start it in the corner. Juan was a willing teacher and was more than happy to give me the kind of instruction that a Jedi master might pass on to his apprentice. He went on to explain that you start the fire in the centre of the stone table in order to warm the area where you will be cooking before transferring it to the corner. He then began a process of dragging red hot coals from the fire into the centre of the stone table making a thin and even layer over which he placed the cooking grill which measured about 80 cm x 50 cm. On to that he placed several huge pieces of meat, lightly seasoned. There they would stay and cook for about an hour and a half while we sipped wine and nibbled on *empanadas* chatting away in Spanish and English. Periodically, Juan would grab his dragging tool which looked to me like an old-fashioned golf putter and drag more coals out of his fire in the corner across to underneath the cooking grill again, meticulously spreading them across the area sustaining this thin even layer of heat. He explained to me that if you couldn't hold your hand over the grill, then it was too hot. This was barbecuing but not as I had known it. This meat was being slow cooked over the charcoal.

A little later, some local sausages were added to the grill including an Argentinian version of black pudding and eventually the whole feast was brought to the table and the meat was served on wooden boards. It was the most delicious meat: tender, well-seasoned, incredible! It was a lovely way to close out the day and for us to get a genuine feel for some Argentinian culture. Luke and I noted that we didn't start eating until around 10:30pm but took it all in our stride. The feeling of friendship and warmth around the table was exceedingly tangible and real.

Later on, Luke decided he would send the Argentinian scrum-half, Tomas Cubelli a message on Instagram to congratulate him on their fantastic win over the Springboks. One can only imagine what kind of massive celebration the Pumas were involved in at the time. It had only been a third victory in their history against South Africa and to have done it in such style was incredible and in front of a knowledgeable and enthusiastic home crowd was the icing on the cake. To everyone's surprise, this international rugby player, amid all the celebrations and singing that was no doubt going on, took the time to reply immediately to Luke. It was an extraordinary gesture I thought, as did everybody round the table and once again it had a huge effect on Luke's mood and overall state of mind. We were amongst special, special people!

Luke: "Well done today, great win. How many times have you won against South Africa?"

Tomi Cubelli: "Thank you bro. How are you? How is the neck? This is the third time."

Luke: "Yeh, it's getting better. I'm out of hospital today. When I saw the high tackle on you I was thinking oh no he's got a bad neck!"

Tomi Cubelli: "Good to hear. Stay strong mate. I guess you are a bit uncomfortable but everything will settle down. Haha, neck is 100%"

Luke: "Yeh it's nice to see you can still play because I love rugby so much I'd be so sad if I couldn't play anymore."

Tomi Cubelli: "You will for sure. Just focus on recover well now. You will have time."

Luke:" How long did you have off?"

Tomi Cubelli: "One year for test rugby"

Luke: "What about club?"

Tomi Cubelli: "I played at month 6 at club level"

Luke: "That's a long time, how did you manage?"

Tomi Cubelli: "Yes long time. Is hard at the start but then you start to focus in short term goals. Time to take a rest now."

Luke: "Thank you. It's nice to see you recovered well."

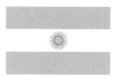 

Mendocino Warmth

The weather in Mendoza at that time of year was absolutely beautiful. We were greeted every morning with the most beautiful clear blue skies, bright sunshine and in most pleasant temperature somewhere in the low 20 degrees centigrade. The next day was no different and the promise of a family lunch outside in the garden with Tano and his son promised to be yet another highlight.

The garden at Juan's house was immaculately kept by his gardener who came two or three times a week to mow grass, trim hedges and prune this and that around the place. Juan told me that it was one of the most difficult places in the world to grow grass. It's effectively like a desert in Mendoza with such low rainfall. For drinking water, they rely entirely on meltwater from the Andes collected in vast reservoirs above the city up in the foothills. In fact, another thing I heard while over there was that in Mendoza, there are no naturally growing trees and every tree in the city was planted deliberately.

So, back at Juan's house there was a swimming pool, though the weather wasn't quite nice enough to put that to full use! I could only imagine in the height of summer, that this place would not only be a haven of tranquillity but a fun spot for swimming and sunbathing. The ever present black and white collie dog was scuffling around chasing the odd bird and barking at passers-by. This dog seemed to take a liking to

Luke and spent a good deal of time in his bedroom. AH! It's come back to me! Luke and I shared a room! I'm not sure to what extent I can blame my ageing years and possible premature onset of senility and subsequent increasingly rubbish memory, or just the traumatic psychological distraction of those events in Mendoza, but I really had forgotten where I had been sleeping!

I had a most pleasant breakfast sat in the garden simply peacefully enjoying the sun and taking a moment to myself to recognise what an incredible experience we were living, in so much as we would never forget it; one that would affect my son in a most meaningful way. He had to do a significant amount of growing up, philosophising and getting his perspectives of life in order. He'd been so fortunate not to have paralysed himself and to have received such wonderful medical attention. In addition, now we were amongst new and caring friends who were dropping everything to ensure we were properly looked after until such time as we could return home.

Later in the morning, Michelle arrived with a large tray of empanadas and a smile! Not long afterwards Tano turned up with an array of meat and sausages and the two of us sat armed with our phones and Google translate apps ready for another stilted, punctuated, slow and faltering conversation. These conversations however were deep, genuine and utterly heartfelt. Tano was clearly one of the most genuine and kind men I've ever met; a man for example, for whom the word *integrity* might have been invented. He more than anyone, as the manager of the U17 team at Los Tordos, wished to finish the job of hosting the Haileybury touring squad well but now his role had taken on a far more personal dimension.

After another long cooking period which I again found fascinating, we sat as a family to eat under the dappled sunlight provided by a pergola. Michelle had brought her two children as had Tano and there was a lovely family feel. The scene itself would not have looked out of place in a painting hanging in the Musée D'Orsay as part of a French Impressionist exhibition of Renoir's most famous pieces. Quite beautiful! Tano was the chef on this occasion and he didn't let us down! The meat was once again served on wooden dishes with some simple salads, this time a potato salad with egg and washed down with more quite spectacular red wine! I have a lovely photo of the occasion and you can tell from a distance the colour of this wine was the deepest darkest red possible. We were then treated to a fantastic dessert; extraordinary ice cream twirled up to look like a cake with chocolate and crushed pecan nuts sprinkled on the top. We were being spoilt all right, that was for sure!

Later that day, Juan took me to a local supermarket where we picked up a few provisions and while there, somewhere down the pasta aisle as I recall, we bumped into the President of another rugby club in the area. Juan introduced me and the gentleman in question already knew about Luke and his predicament and while he spoke no English at all, it was clear that he was wishing Luke a speedy recovery and good luck in the future. Juan was also translating for me and it really was quite heart-warming to know that there were yet more offers of help and support, in this case, from a club we had not even visited! What openness and warmth these *Mendocinos* possessed.

On a complete side note, I found out later that Cesar was also an architect and one that specialised in designing supermarkets. In fact, he had designed the supermarket that we had been in that evening! I was also getting the impression that Mendoza was one of these quite small cities where everyone seemed to know everyone. Cesar himself had been in touch and had invited us to lunch the next day. I couldn't wait.

He arrived as planned late the next morning full of the joys of life! He was an emotional man and not afraid to show it. A man after my own heart! We hopped into the car, drove through the various quiet streets of this gated community we found ourselves in, out through the security gates that resembled something you might find outside a secretive CIA installation and off into the streets beyond. We were heading to Cesar's son's school to pick him up and head off for lunch. The school itself was spread over a large area and it looked to have excellent facilities for sport and learning. We headed up to Cesar's house to drop off a couple of things and once again we found ourselves approaching another security gate as we entered his compound. Each of these houses was very different in design, but were also incredibly stylish and individual. It came as no surprise when Cesar told me that he had designed his own house. Why wouldn't he? He was an architect! So we drove around and had a little guided visit of the city with its park and fancy gates, with all along Cesar giving his very best impression of a tourist guide. In all fairness, he was very knowledgeable. He had mentioned the possibility of taking us to the stadium where the Pumas had beaten South Africa two days before. Thus we found ourselves driving up the avenue towards the main entrance and a security guard in a little box peering out at us through his glass window. There was a brief exchange in Spanish where it seemed clear the security guard had no real inclination to allow Cesar to drive through. Cesar on the other hand had other plans. His part of the conversation seemed more persuasive and appeared to press home a point of view which although I didn't understand, seemed to have the desired effect in that we entered the stadium! I'm not entirely sure the security guard had much in the way of choice as, if my recollection is not failing, Cesar's car didn't actually come to an exact standstill at any point. So we were in! He then drove all the way to the main entrance to the stadium and parked his car right outside. In what seemed to me to be a wonderfully Latin disregard for rules and regulations, he left his car exactly where he wanted, meaning for the shortest walk possible to the stadium, on this occasion approximately 20 metres.

So Luke and I, along with Cesar and his son Julio, are now walking up the steps into the main entrance. As we go in, a man walks towards us who clearly recognises Cesar. Warm greetings all round followed, as this gentleman, who worked for the local government on some kind of sports committee, was the father of Cesar's son's girlfriend! I mentioned earlier about a small city?! So good news: we weren't going to be kicked out! Quite the contrary in fact as now we had been invited for a proper guided tour and all sorts of doors opened! We were taken down into the dressing rooms to be shown where the players had been changing only days before and this gentleman pointed to a seat in the corner and told Luke and I that this is where Lionel Messi sits when Argentina play at the ground. I confess to be not that interested in soccer, but I know Luke was pretty impressed; in all fairness I thought it was pretty cool too! We left the changing room, were guided down some steps and out onto the field of play. The ground was entirely empty. The rugby goals had already gone and been replaced with football goals and the groundsmen were busy going about their business. It was another wonderful experience walking around the ground. It had been built for the 1978 football World Cup hosted by Argentina and all I knew about the ground apart from its rather politically driven naming, was that it was the location for Scotland's most famous goal scored by Archie Gemmill against Holland during that particular World Cup. A photo opportunity with Luke in that goal mouth was not passed up! I had remembered the goal from its rather humorous appearance in the film *Trainspotting* and have since watched it many times on YouTube. Fair play to Mr Gemmill, it's a pretty good goal!

Afterwards we found a place to eat within a beautiful park and we sat outside enjoying the sun and pleasant atmosphere. Faced with the prospect of eating more meat, as I glanced down the menu, my eyes were drawn to what I thought I might have at first been imagining – a salad section! I actually quite fancied it and ordered a chicken Caesar salad with a side order of fries. I forget what Luke had but if I was a betting man, a burger would not be far down my list of likely candidates. We'd spent yet another lovely day with new friends in a beautiful city and Luke's recuperation was starting in the very best possible manner.

On another occasion, Tano offered to take Luke and I up into the mountains for something of a trip in order to blow the cobwebs and take in some of the fantastic surrounding scenery. He picked us up in his four-wheel-drive with a young man from the rugby club. This chap had evidently convinced Tano that he need not be at school that afternoon. I was sceptical but it was none of my business! As we drove out of the city, so the scenery became more and more impressive. As we followed the path of a river that over tens of thousands of years had carved an impressive valley into the mountain, we pulled over for a photo opportunity. We continued to climb into the foothills of the Andes. Tano was a knowledgeable tour guide and I became glad that not only

Luke had some teenage company but this young man was doing a good job translating Tano's informative commentary. He told us about how the area obtains and maintains its supply of drinking water, essentially meltwater from the Andes through a system of dams and reservoirs. He spoke about the inevitable destruction of a number of villages in order to create such reservoirs. We drove through a lengthy tunnel and as we exited were greeted with the most stunning scene: a beautiful flat lake, vast in size, set amongst huge jagged mountains all bathed in sunlight. Once again we pulled over for a stroll and a few photos. We walked down the road that eventually was submerged by the water level. I'm one of these people who when faced with a body of flat water cannot resist the temptation to search for appropriately shaped stones and attempt a world record for skimming! This occasion was no different and thankfully there were a number of suitable candidates lying all around me. The scene was absolutely beautiful with reeds along the edge of the water and local birds not dissimilar to our moorhens all around. I was having some success with my skimming but on one occasion, I'm ashamed to say, an ill directed throw, pulled significantly to the left, managed to hit one of these birds. He had been floating around on the surface with a few birdmates, just minding his own business. There was a puff of feathers into the air as the bird then took off in something of a huff. I guess that was fair enough. Had I been doing it on purpose I would have felt like something of a Jedi Master bird-hunter; however as it was, I was a bit embarrassed and certainly felt sorry for the bird.

On the way back down the mountain we stopped off at a rather fancy hotel over-looking the lake. It was a lovely spot to have a coffee and a hot chocolate and a good chat before heading home. I recall Tano playing a joke on Luke, who had been chatting with Celeste on the phone. As he made his way over to the table, Tano had prepared one of those children's highchairs to sit on. The irony of course is that Luke's giant frame could barely fit in one of the normal chairs let alone this tiddly little highchair. It was what I might call a *chucklesome* moment.

We had some nice outings during our time and it was clear our Mendocino friends were keen to show a little of their region, spoil Luke and ensure that we did not get too stir crazy at Juan's house. We had a lovely lunch one day with Juan and Micha at a shopping mall in Mendoza. We ate outside on a beautiful day and were treated once again to gorgeous food. After the meal we passed an amusement arcade and I remember Luke getting excited at the site of a *Walking Dead* 'shoot'em up' game. Juan, with no hesitation at all, set off and returned quickly with a fully charged up game token card for Luke to fill his boots. As Luke began to play, we watched on with great joy and I could tell that Juan was taking particular pleasure in watching Luke enjoying himself like a teenage boy and taking his mind entirely off his situation, for a while at least. Juan was like one of those grandparents who simply loved spoiling their grandchildren and seeing them happy.

On his return from the Stadium visit with Cesar, Luke was very tired, his neck was still obviously quite sore and stiff and his hip was still giving him plenty of pain. He was still walking with some discomfort and taking pain relief on a regular basis. At the time, we were still unsure as to when we would be going home but were reasonably hopeful that it would be some time that week. We would find out more the next day as we were due to see Mr Terraza back at the *Clinica Francesa* for what we hoped would be our last visit.

Going Home

On Tuesday morning, we had our final consultation with the surgeon and it was hoped that he would be giving us the good news with an *all clear* to travel home and in some small way return to normal life. After a quick bite of breakfast, the ever willing Juan took us back to the Clinica Francesa. We were beginning to recognise the roads and features of Mendoza with its generally arid feel but magnificent surrounding mountains. We parked up around the corner where the usual small amount of money was passed over to an awaiting youth. I wish I had asked Juan what that money was for. Certainly the car didn't get washed, so I was left speculating that this was some kind of scam, an understood agreement, that this gentleman (and I use the word in its absolute broadest sense as no gentleman would dress like this young man nor hang out on street corners and keep the kind of company this chap did) would in some way watch over the car and ensure its security during our time in the hospital. Shady stuff, I thought.

It was strangely nice to be back in the clinic with its air-conditioning and clean surfaces and above all friendly staff. We did not wait long before being invited into a small room to meet with Mr Terraza. He was brilliant once again and tried to explain the situation in his best English but as Juan was there, the surgeon also made good use of his grasp of English. He examined Luke, asked plenty of questions and finally explained that it would indeed be possible for Luke to return to the UK. Cesar was also at the hospital to hear the good news although he had not come into the consultation room. He was waiting down below at reception. Mr Terraza signed some paperwork, the all-important paperwork for the insurance company, there was handshaking and hugs and once again my eyes filled with emotion. I had noticed from the start that these medical professionals who had taken such great care of Luke were far more emotionally open than would be the case in the UK. That's not to take anything away from the professional aspect of British or Argentinian staff. In our time, we've had excellent care from both. However, it's worth noting that it seemed to mean more to these folks in Mendoza. We were treated like friends and family, not customers or patients. Perhaps that was down to the unusual and particular circumstances of Luke being a young Englishman, or a rugby player, or the connections with Los Tordos Rugby Club. Who knows, but my observations were unambiguous.

We packed away the paperwork with great care and took the lift downstairs to the reception where Cesar was waiting. Juan headed off to work and Cesar would take us home. The rest of the day was spent communicating with Pitu, Angus and the school as we tried to map the next few days and how that would play out. We were still entirely uncertain as to how we would return home and particularly when we would fly. In theory we were ready to go though Mr Terraza had indicated more rest would be beneficial.

Communication with the insurance company had not been that fluid, though I know Pitu and Angus had been doing a sterling job trying to stir up some action. I had e-mailed my boss, The Master at Haileybury, in order to explain the situation and had received a number of reassuring, supportive and kind e-mails. In fact, I had also received a message of support from the Chairman of Governors, Alan Pilgrim, himself the father of a keen sportsman and I could tell he was very much concerned; it was good to receive his support. For years I had pooh-poohed modern technology but my goodness, this whole exercise in Mendoza would have been an entirely different operation without the use of my phone. Just receiving the odd friendly text message was a real boost, of course communicating with my wife Celeste had been crucial throughout, the "Luke in Mendoza" group chat and access to my e-mails were all critical elements of me successfully managing this situation. So I reluctantly bow down and accept how useful the smart phone is. I never thought I would hear myself say that! In fact I will go as far as to say *how on earth did we ever manage before?!*

That evening, Luke and I were invited to the rugby club to watch some training as the team were preparing for a match the following day. It was our first return to LTRC since Luke's injury and I wasn't entirely sure how he would react. On arrival, training was already underway, but there was a handful of parents on touchlines who greeted us with great warmth. Mothers I hadn't met giving me great big hugs, lots of handshakes and kisses and again much Mendocino warmth. As had been the case throughout the whole ordeal, Luke took the whole exercise in his stride. Perhaps he enjoyed the attention. We strolled over to watch what seemed like a very purposeful warm-up over on the U17 pitch, and sat down on a patch of pale, dry grass......which was pretty much the whole ground, other than the 1st XV pitch. We watched intently and one of the coaches came over to shake hands and congratulated Luke on his progress. The entire conversation was in Spanish but I'm fairly sure that that was the gist of it. Los Tordos Rugby Club is also a women's hockey club and it wasn't too long before three enthusiastic teenage hockey players had made their way around the field to meet this English chap that everybody seemed to be talking about. Conversations between teenage boys and teenage girls can often be nervy occasions and the chat is not always free-flowing. Imagine the scene between three girls who spoke no English, and I mean not a single word, and a young man who spoke no Spanish. It was painful to watch though I sympathised with all parties. I tried to explain a few facts in my improving Spanish but I too ran aground fairly quickly. It was sad really as the girls I think simply wanted to meet Luke and have a chitchat out of interest with a young man from a different part of the world. It wasn't long before they cut their losses, said goodbye and about turned to head off up the touchline. Not long after, Luke and I were joined by an owl. An unusual sight for both of us but this owl had also decided to take an interest in the rugby session. It flew over and perched on a fence post about 20 m from us and sat there taking in the scene. I wondered what possible interest this would be to a predatory bird. Perhaps it was analysing the session and might offer some feedback to the coaches at the end. I wonder how that might have sounded?

Owl: "okay I thought that was a really good session coach, but have you thought of introducing games in which the players can develop their skills under more pressure of time and space and in doing so, introduce a decision-making process too?"

After training, we were invited for a drink at the clubhouse. The clubhouse at LTRC has a warm welcoming feel and like many clubhouses around the world, is adorned with rugby memorabilia, team photos both modern and ancient, various shields, trophies, shirts of all shapes and sizes and of course, a well-stocked bar. As we sat down for a beer with Tano, he mentioned that the beer we were drinking was made by him. I was sat next to an architect who in his spare time ran a small brasserie! And this bottled beer was seriously good! My mind went back to a conversation with Juan when he explained that while he was in finance he also had a small acreage of vineyards growing the famous Malbec grape. When I asked how much he produced his response was "around 150,000kgs a year." I've no idea how much that is in reality but it sounded more than a small acreage!

Tano was kind enough to order some food for us all and once again there was no question of me putting my hand in my pocket for any of this. Luke and I commented on a number of occasions about how late in the evening training was and meals were. This was no exception! It was now about 10:30 in the evening and we were waiting for our home-made pizza to arrive which we would wash down with Tano's very own brew. The players were beginning to filter back from the showers to the clubhouse and they were all greeting Luke with great affection and in varying degrees of recognisable English, but mostly in Spanish or *Castellano* as it is known. They were all keen to hear of his progress and there was much hugging and tapping of shoulders, though as Luke was still wearing his collar, they were all going gently! In fact, one of the reasons we were told Luke had to continue wearing a collar was to give a clear message to those around him. Indeed, the surgeon explained that the metal plate screwed into his C3 and C5 would be enough to secure the area and that the wearing of the collar was predominantly to protect the stitches and incision wound while it was healing.

One of the most delicious pizzas I've ever eaten (possibly because by now I was absolutely starving) arrived at the table with ham, cheese and sliced pickles. Absolutely gorgeous! We all tucked in with great enthusiasm, and after a very brief but purposeful discussion, another was ordered! Eventually the evening ground to a halt, we said our goodbyes and were dropped off at our new home by Tano.

It was great to be in a rugby environment - an unmistakable atmosphere - and we were invited to the match the following evening which Luke and I were both very much looking forward to.

My recollection of the next day is dominated by administrative tasks. I was still very anxious about the challenges of starting a new academic year both in the language department and in my boarding house. These things just don't happen by themselves and preparing to welcome around 60 boys back for a new school year is daunting at the best of times let alone when you find yourself on a different continent with just days to go. In the run-up to a new academic year, there are always a number of meetings and training sessions to attend. I remained preoccupied by the fact that I was likely not to be able to attend my tutor group meeting. This is a meeting when the housemaster welcomes his team for an hour or so in preparation for the big return. For the first time, our tutor team consisted of seven tutors all needing to be briefed up on the new year, some key events of the summer like exam results and plans for dealing with the upcoming challenges. There was no way I could expect my new Assistant Housemaster, Peter Bromfield, himself new to the school, to lead this meeting. Thus I turned to Angus MacDonald who was still doing sterling work liaising with our school insurance company. I was glad to have Angus not only on the tour team but also in my tutor team. I began writing up some notes for the new term simply handwritten on blank pieces of paper in the pad that Juan had brought to me in the hospital for me to sketch on. Having only done one drawing the whole time, there were plenty of sheets left upon which to scribble my meeting notes. Having completed my notes in my very best handwriting, something we are increasingly not used to, I photographed every page and sent them to poor Angus via my phone and apologetically thanked him for going ahead and running the meeting set for that Friday. By all accounts Angus did a great job and I was grateful from where I was sitting to know that he had been so willing to help me out once again.

Later that day I made my one and only phone call to the insurance company. That was the measure of what a fantastic job Angus, Pitu and Pancho had done between them to liaise with both the UK office and Buenos Aires office of the insurance companies. I had been able to focus fully on Luke and I will be eternally grateful for their efforts. On this occasion, however, frustrated with the lack of news, I phoned to find out what the situation was. I got a story about waiting for *this information*, or expecting to receive *that confirmation*. It was all very dull and irritating. The delay was largely due to the fact that the insurance company was insisting that Luke and I returned home with a medical escort despite the fact that Luke seemed to be in perfectly good shape. This was adding days to our stay in Mendoza. I learned that the plan was to fly a qualified agency medical escort down from Miami to join us in Mendoza before accompanying Luke on his flight to Buenos Aires, then on to Heathrow and then in a taxi directly to our front door. It did seem like overkill to me but I appreciated that the insurance company were taking no risks and at the end of the day, Luke had been through a serious surgical procedure just a week before. If any readers want to know exactly what Luke went through, one can easily find a corporectomy video on YouTube!

That evening, we returned to the rugby club to watch the game the boys had been preparing so diligently for the previous day. Astonishingly, it was a 9pm kick-off which we were beginning to get used to. The Los Tordos boys played extremely well and were better than their visitors in most departments. Their set scrum was in particularly dominating form and around the park their breakdown work and support play was exceptional. They played with a level of ambition matched by their skill set and as a result the game was most entertaining. There was a very decent crowd most likely down to the fact that both teams seemed to have huge squads. The home team, our new club, had a vast bench and rolling subs. Once again we retired to the clubhouse after the game for a few more drinks and some food, some very late food! Luke and I remarked to each other how extraordinarily late the evenings were and that these boys were supposedly getting up in the morning to go to school.

On this occasion, guided by our good friend Tano, we ordered the Milanesa. This was a large flattened out very thin but very large piece of beef covered in breadcrumbs and herbs, with a layer of delicious tomato sauce and topped with cheese. Served with chips, this was an absolute delight! After our meal there was time for a few photos with the boys and Luke as this would certainly be our last visit to Los Tordos Rugby Club. It had become a tremendous lifeboat of a place that Luke and I will never forget!

By the end of that day, we had received confirmation that we would fly home on the Friday and that the day before, our nurse from Miami, Penny would meet us at Juan's home to get to know us, check on Luke and answer any questions we might have. So we had much to look forward to and when Penny arrived that Thursday, she was obviously extremely experienced and seemed like a lovely lady to boot. She explained that she had been doing this kind of work for years and revealed some extraordinary number of miles that she had covered the previous year. Above all else, she struck me as very professional and caring towards Luke which was all I could ask for. She pulled forth from her bag a range of gadgets which she used to check on Luke's vital signs and thankfully, apart from his injury, he was in tiptop condition. She told us what time she would be around in the morning before asking if we had any further questions. At this point I explained to her that I had a letter from the surgeon clearly stating that Luke should travel first class and that I should travel first class alongside him. I asked therefore how the travel arrangements would work. Given the length of the flight from Buenos Aires to Heathrow, I was absolutely desperate to jump on this first-class bandwagon! She paused before responding as if in some way, she had been asked this question 1000 times before and couldn't quite believe she was being asked it again. Her response was short and to the point. "Carl…Luke travels first-class, I travel first class, *you* travel economy!" Luke was sat on the sofa laughing like someone who had never heard a joke before, had never even been made aware of the concept of humour and had been deliberately deprived of anything remotely funny for the entirety of his soon to be 16 years of life. Not that I am still bitter!

To my great joy, Juan explained that for Luke's last evening in Mendoza he would host an *asado* and was inviting some key people along like Tano, Cesar, Pancho and to my great surprise, Pitu. He lived in Buenos Aires, and had decided to fly to Mendoza to make the first leg of our trip with us the next day, despite the fact that it would fly him straight back to Buenos Aires. He also knew one of Juan's pals from LTRC, a rugby journalist called Juan Pablo Garcia who was also attending the barbecue. It was such a lovely evening. It started as all of these events do with a glass or two of wonderful wine and a really nice chat while the meat slowly cooked on its grill. What a wonderful bunch of fellows all coming together to support this young English kid they hadn't known a week before. Our flight the next day was leaving at around 6:30 in the morning and we knew that Penny would be knocking on the door at 4am. Ouch! Despite that, the lengthy process of cooking the meal and chit chatting away meant that at around 10:30pm, we were just about considering sitting down and eating. Despite the meaningful but relaxed nature of the occasion, I had butterflies throughout. I was not only feeling very emotional, but had decided to attempt a thank you speech in Spanish, a language I had never spoken prior to our arrival in Mendoza. However, fast progress had been made with the help of Google translate, my Spanish verbs app on the phone and frequent guidance and support from my new friends. They were not only helping Luke recover from his injury but also giving me the odd linguistic nudge and as a French teacher, I was open to such nudges! Cesar, who had agreed to see us off at the airport the next day because his son was catching a flight to Brazil with some buddies at around the same time, had to leave early and this was my cue to launch into action. While I spoke from the heart, I still tried my best to produce some accurate verbs and even the odd appropriate use of the infinitive. The GCSE exam boards I think would have been impressed! I spoke about the exceptional support that we had received that made a potentially catastrophic situation for us reasonably manageable. I spoke about new friendships and a new family. I spoke about the undeniable strength of the bond of rugby players wherever you find yourself in the world. I suppose it was a thank you speech with a difference.

I managed to get to the end, just about, without breaking down; however, glancing around the table, by the time I had finished, all I could see was a collection of grown men in their 40s and 50s with their eyes welling up, but gleaming with pride and a sense of achievement. Pitu on the other hand had something of a different look as I had not seen him for well over a week. Somehow in that time I had gone from not speaking Spanish to delivering an emotional thank you in his own language. He had tears in his eyes like the rest of them, but he also had a look of surprise which I quite liked. Before Cesar left, they presented us with a couple of books about LTRC. In a typical gesture that Luke and I were getting used to, we opened the books to find everyone had written a personal note to myself and Luke; a wonderful souvenir that barely scratches the surface in terms of representing the extraordinary experience through which we had had the privilege to go. In fact, apart from Luke's injury, every other experience had been exceptionally positive, memorable, heart-warming and Luke particularly, learnt a lot about people ......and himself.

So after about four hours of sleep, we were up, packed, and ready to go. Right on 4am, there was a knock at the door and Penny was standing there with her travel case and a *let's get cracking* look on her face. We all jumped into Juan's car, drove down the very quiet private streets and through the security gates for the last time. At that time of the morning it didn't take long to arrive at the airport where we checked in for the shortish hop to Buenos Aires. We sat and drank a few coffees and ate some pastries and after not too long we were joined by Cesar. We were surprised to see him arrive by himself as we knew his son was travelling at the same time as Luke and I. Cesar explained that he had got his son's flight times wrong and that he was flying much later in the day. I was astonished that despite his error, Cesar had got up at this ungodly hour to see us off anyway. Even at this late stage, the Mendocinos were going well, well out of their way to show their care for us. I'll never forget it.

Such was the commitment of LTRC to do a good job that Cesar had in fact been tasked to write up a report of the whole incident. I thought this spoke volumes about the kind of organisation the club was. I believe the idea was that Cesar would look at all the circumstances and how their club responded with a view to preparing more thoroughly should such an injury occur again. I know that Los Tordos frequently welcomes young touring rugby teams from around the world and so it came as no surprise to find out that this report, reflective but forward-looking as it would be, was being compiled. I have no doubt at all that Cesar did a first-class job. Perhaps one day when my Spanish is up to it, I'll ask to read a copy.

Eventually it was time for us to go through to the departure area and so we said our emotional goodbyes and more thank yous and made promises to stay in touch. I'm glad to say that we have indeed stayed in touch with the good people of Mendoza and Los Tordos Rugby Club.

The flight to Buenos Aires was uneventful and mercifully brief particularly as I felt sorry for Luke in his collar but despite that he did seem reasonably comfortable. Buenos Aires airport was busy but Luke and I were ably guided by not only Pitu but also Penny, who seemed to have travelled the world alongside various injured people from across the globe. We were in good hands! When we arrived at the British Airways check-in desk I was absolutely blown away when the lady behind the desk greeted us with "Ah, you must be the young Englishman who had the accident." Mendoza is 985 km from Buenos Aires! What on earth was going on? There was no putting off for any longer, an emotional goodbye with Pitu. Huge thanks were due to this man who had become a good friend with remarkable warmth of spirit, genuine care and love. It might seem that I am using such words too superficially, however I am confident that their use in this case, is wholly appropriate.

So leaving Pitu behind us and following Penny like a couple of little ducklings, we made our way to the first-class lounge. I have no idea how she managed to convince the stern faced security operator manning the door to allow me in with my rather flimsy economy ticket, but she did. I'm sorry to say that Luke and I were a little awestruck by the whole experience. Free food? Free booze? I think it's safe to say that we weren't used to that kind of treatment and we made the most of it. So we ate, and we drank and Luke was delighted to be able to watch some football on a giant screen. When we boarded our flight, there was more hilarity as Luke was guided towards his business class seat/recliner as I was herded back to the economy pen. I tried to convince myself how good it was to see Luke laughing. I didn't try all that hard. We then discovered that remarkably, there was one free seat in the whole of the business class area and it was right next to Luke and Penny. I could not believe my luck and so requests were made for me to be upgraded. I did not think that this was an unreasonable request given that my son was travelling business class, in his collar and after his major surgery! For some inexplicable reason my request was turned down. We later found out that due to a problem on another business class seat, a lady was moved to that spare seat. That did little to improve my mood.

Penny had been fantastic throughout the whole trip not only providing the obvious medical reassurance but it was like travelling with one's parents again, with very little to concern myself with. She led from the front and dealt with admin, passport checks and so on. She even expertly homed in on the driver who was waiting for us at Heathrow arrivals to take us home. We also bumped into a friend, Dave Phillips at arrivals. He appears again later in this story. We got into a very comfortable black Mercedes and were very much looking forward to arriving home and seeing our family. He drove us right to our front door and we arrived back at

Haileybury at around 9am on the Saturday morning. In another extraordinary coincidence or phenomenal piece of luck, as we arrived, the senior rugby squad who had been on tour with us were meeting at the Pavilion for the start of a pre-season rugby session. It was a beautiful day, with blue sky and not a breath of wind. It was just perfect. The boys from the squad had not seen Luke since he had been taken away in the ambulance the day of his injury and so they were incredibly pleased to see him and vice versa. The boys hugged, gently, and they were full of questions. It was a freakishly timed reunion but a very welcome coincidence or twist of fate.

We then rang the front door and of course Celeste rushed out and held him tentatively but lovingly. We said goodbye and thank you to Penny, taking an obligatory souvenir photo before she got back in her black chauffeur-driven Mercedes to head off to her hotel near Heathrow prior to her flying home the next day. What an extraordinary lifestyle. I could see then how it would be easy for her to total up the kind of air miles she had spoken about that Thursday. It was the end of a very long journey that had begun three weeks before with our flight to Chile. Luke and I had both returned, changed men, and he in particular had done an extraordinary amount of growing up. He had needed to of course, but he had been shown so many rich and appealing human qualities along the way that he could not fail to have grown as a person himself.

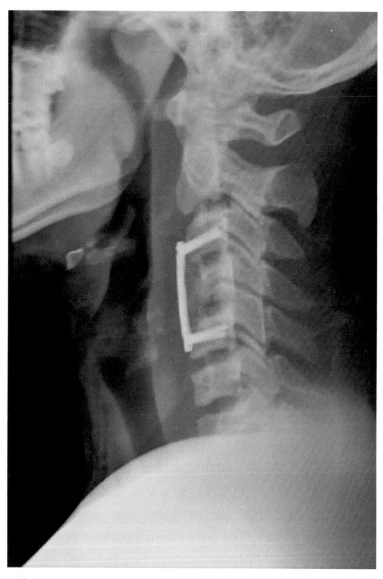

The metal plate screwed into Luke's C3 and C5 vertebrae
will stay there forever. And no, it doesn't set off the airport
security metal detector alarm!

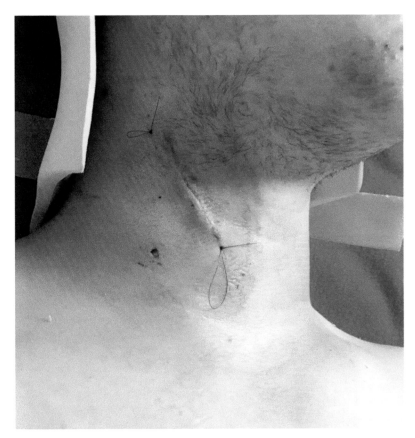

Luke's scar healed really well over the next year or so.

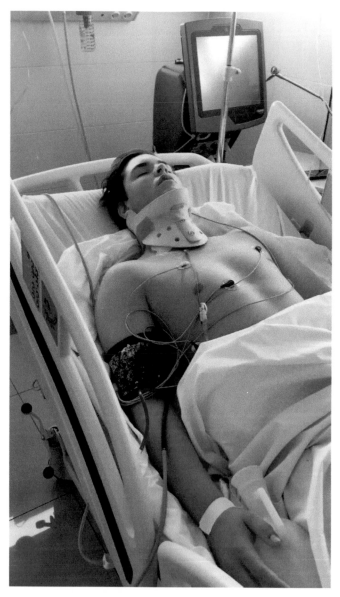

Luke in the Intensive Care Unit, the morning after his
surgery.

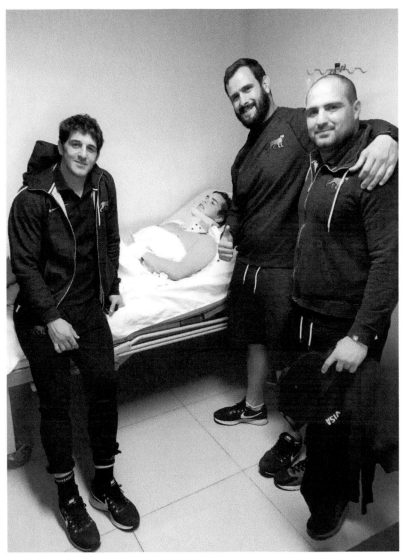

The visit of the three Pumas was a real highlight and
energised Luke for a range of reasons.

New friends and family. A memorable and relaxing time.
A lunchtime *asado* in Juan's garden.

Above: Tano and I at the lake, I think, just after I had hit that bird!
Below: An *asado* at Juan's house, just getting going.

Above: Mr Terraza signing Luke fit to leave the country and fly back to the UK.

Top right: My one and only sketch during my time: Luke's 'receptacle' (empty).

Bottom Right: Some new friends at LTRC.

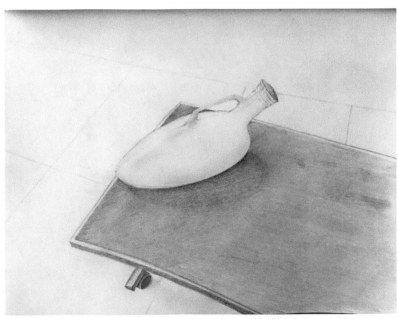

Below: Penny and Luke at our front door – end of a long journey.

Top left: The last supper, Pancho can be seen top left with Tano, Juan and Cesar kneeling at the front.

Bottom left: Pitu, Luke and I at the airport in Buenos Aires, just before saying goodbye.

We managed, one way or another, to get Luke back on the
morning of his 16th Birthday!

Back to School

One thing that had been playing on my mind for some time during our stay in Mendoza was that not only was I feeling under some self-generated pressure to return to Haileybury in time to begin the new academic year, despite the Master's supportive reassurances, but also that September 1st was Luke's birthday. The day we arrived back at Haileybury was Saturday, September 1st. Celeste of course, had been told exactly when we would arrive and had set up our traditional birthday morning present opening session. This normally involves putting a happy birthday banner up in the lounge, something we have been doing since the boys were tiny and laying out birthday presents on the coffee table. Preparations on that day were no different but there was certainly a very different feel about the occasion. Firstly, we'd made it! Secondly, it was a family reunion with a difference and there was more to celebrate than just Luke's 16th birthday. Luke opened his presents and spent the rest of the day catching up on sleep and resting, as did I. In the evening, however, we were able to go out for a family meal during which I asked the waitress to take a photo of us as a family which I instantly posted on the 'Luke in Mendoza' WhatsApp group. The guys back in Mendoza were delighted and I detected a very real sense of closure and feeling of a job well done; they had successfully delivered us home in time for Luke's birthday.

Luke had a few more days of rest before returning to school. What ended up being incredible was that other than a handful of consultant visits, Luke didn't miss a day of school. He had been clearly instructed to continue wearing the collar for the first three weeks of school which he duly did. On his first day back, he put on his uniform, put on his collar and cracked on as if nothing had happened. Once again I had a huge sense of pride as Luke impressed me with his philosophical approach and can do/will do attitude. "It is what it is", he would say to me often. During his first week back it did become clear however that he was getting tired very quickly. The school day at Haileybury is a busy and exhausting one, not least because of the fact that each pupil covers a number of kilometres of walking each day simply to get to and from their lessons, such is the scale of the campus. It was agreed therefore, that once Luke's lessons had finished, he would return home to rest. Luke was fortunate in that as I am a housemaster, he lives right in the centre of the campus; just a short walk for him therefore to and from school, and by short I mean about 50m! He would take no part in any sporting activity or indeed any other co-curricular exercise. His time in the CCF was certainly, for the time being, cut short. As for any sporty young man, this period of inactivity became a source of real frustration. He was still during the early stages, getting a good deal of pain from his hip, but as that pain dissipated so the frustration grew as he was not able to play with his friends. Such is the set-up at school, one sees one's friends disappearing off after lunch, getting changed and heading off to the football fields or rugby fields to have some fun. Sights like these did nothing to raise Luke's morale. At times therefore, he appeared very low and would occasionally snap back at me if I was trying to make some point about his progress or indeed about the amount of time he would spend lying on his bed playing Fifa. On one occasion, in tears with frustration, he shouted at me. I realised at that point where Luke's mind was and gave some thought to how we might address the situation.

My mind was drawn back to the wonderful moment when three Argentinian internationals walked into Luke's hospital room to meet with him. One of those players, Juan Figallo was on the books at Saracens. Haileybury has a long and happy relationship with Saracens rugby club. Chris Wyles was an U16 in my first year at Haileybury back in September 1999 and he went on to play several hundred times for Saracens and represented the United States in a number of world cups and sevens competitions. In fact, in 2015, the USA Eagles chose Haileybury as a base at which to train for a couple of weeks during the Rugby World Cup. They came shortly after Argentina in fact. In a wonderful twist therefore, Chris Wyles was able to return to Haileybury as captain of the Eagles. In addition, Saracen Jamie George, by now an England International and British Lion was educated at Haileybury as was the exciting young forward Nick Isiekwe. Jonathan George, Jamie's older brother is part of the physio team and their father Ian, the former Director of Sport and 1st XV coach at Haileybury, also has a role with some of the academy players. Our current Director of Rugby, former Wales captain and British Lion, Michael Owen also had a spell at Saracens. In addition, a couple of years before, I had a talented young scrum-half in Lawrence, my boarding house, called Bryn McCall. He was the son of the Saracens Director of Rugby, Mark McCall. I had an idea that I might ask Mark a small favour.

Juan Figallo had struck me as a fantastic bloke when we met in Luke's hospital room a few weeks before. I also knew that he had had the same kind of fusion surgery on his vertebrae that Luke had undergone and since then had returned to playing top-flight rugby. He had been extremely encouraging with Luke and I wondered if he would be prepared to mentor Luke during what promised to be a long and patient period of rehabilitation. I knew that Saracens trained at St Albans which is only half an hour away so I tried my luck. I had Mark McCall's e-mail address which was perfectly normal as he was a former parent and sent him a message explaining what had happened to Luke and asking his thoughts on my request to involve Juan as his mentor. Once I sent Mark's e-mail, I simply got on with some work in my office. Three minutes later I received an e-mail from Juan Figallo himself. I actually couldn't believe it and stared at the bold line at the top of my outlook inbox for a while before eventually clicking on it:

"Hi Carl how are you?

I'm currently in Argentina but I'll be back next week so, give me a call next week and we can plan something together that what we can do to help Luke in the best way.
I'm happy to help with everything.
See you soon
Till next week.
*My phone: 07*** ******
Juan"

This was a very exciting development, of course. I really felt that this could be a serious lift for Luke and perhaps just the tonic he needed to get mentally back on track and recognise that what he was going through was not forever and that there would be an achievable end goal. He had to be patient. I knew Juan Figallo was going through a period of rehab, a lengthy one in fact, after a serious knee injury. I waited as instructed and then contacted Juan on his return from Argentina. I invited him over for lunch to Haileybury and the three of us sat down in Haileybury's beautiful Dining Hall chatting about rugby, injuries, patience, Saracens, Argentina…everything. There was a real sparkle in Luke's eyes; the first I'd seen for some time. I was hugely grateful to this professional and international rugby player for taking time out to support Luke. We stopped in the Quad for a souvenir photo on our way back to Lawrence, had a coffee, then I accompanied Juan back to his car. Two things rested firmly in my mind after he left. He strongly recommended that we contacted Jonathan George at Saracens. As I mentioned earlier, Jonathan was one of the 1st team physios but what I hadn't known was that Jonathan was responsible for Juan Figallo's rehab and recovery after his fusion surgery. Juan could not speak highly enough of the work that Jonathan had done with him and I considered it to be good advice and acted on it immediately. The second thing that stuck in my mind was this comment:

"If you want to return, your neck has got to be freaking strong!"

It didn't leave too much room for manoeuvre. The clarity of this expression struck me deeply.

During this time, I had also received a few messages of support from Dean Holder at the Injured Players Foundation. We discussed a possible visit so that he could meet Luke and me but in the end, for no particular reason, that meeting never materialised. It wasn't, however, the last I would hear from the IPF. We were now in the process of being referred to a consultant. Despite the fact that Luke had undergone a successful surgical procedure in Argentina, it was always going to be necessary to have him seen in the UK to follow up and monitor his progress. Would the metalwork hold? Would the neurological effects dissipate? Would new bone begin to grow? All these questions needed answering.

We had our first consultation with Mr Ahmed at the Princess Alexandra Hospital in Harlow. We were seen extremely promptly and sent for an x-ray. Mr Ahmed was very happy with what he saw. The issue of the neurological problems was a continued cause for concern. Luke was still feeling tingling sensations down his right arm and some numbness at the ends of his fingers. Mr Ahmed was very reassuring, suggesting that nerves take some time to recover and that he felt confident that over the next few months these feelings would improve and eventually disappear entirely. Total rest was required for the time being, but he did offer us an idea of the long-term plan for a return to physical activity. It was set out clearly month by month so Luke and I could now not only look forward to him progressing but also make plans. Luke had to wait several months before he could start cycling in the gym, then some months later some light jogging before a possible return to some sport around May. That would coincide with the summer non-contact rugby sessions that Michael Owen runs at school and was a clear focal point towards which Luke could aim.

Jonathan George and his identical twin Gareth were both pupils at Haileybury. When I joined, back in September 1999 their father Ian George was housemaster of Batten house, 1st XV coach and Director of Sport. I was beginning my fourth year of teaching and that first term, I shared the U16A team with the Head of PE, Paul Strike, himself a former Saracen who ended up leaving teaching to run his own business, a very successful diving company called Fourth Element. Coincidentally, Chris Wyles was a player in that U16 team. I had shared the coaching duties for my first four seasons as a teacher but the following season in September 2000, I ran the U15A team by myself. It was my first experience of having my own team and it turned out to be a memorable one. It was a great bunch of players and to this day, it is the only team photograph that I have kept. The mount in which the photograph sits is signed by all the players and proudly sat in the front row were two twins, Jonathan and Gareth George. I remember also one summer, Celeste and I were moving house from one school accommodation to another. The distance between the two houses was about 70 metres so we considered moving ourselves with the help of a borrowed flatbed van from the school. On that occasion we also summoned the services of two young fit and strong fellows named Jonathan and Gareth who were only too pleased to assist for some pocket money. Following Juan Figallo's advice, I had contacted Jonathan and was now about to meet him in his capacity as a grown man and a professional.

On our arrival at Old Albanians RFC, where Saracens base their training, we pulled up and parked in the car park surrounded by Saracens branded vehicles. I could already sense that this would be quite exciting for Luke. Jonathan met us outside and it was great to see him. He walked us into the physiotherapy area and we sat down in the first instance for a chat. I was immediately struck by how phenomenally professional Jonathan was. I was also reassured to hear that not only had Jonathan successfully rehabbed Juan Figallo, but also recent arrival Chris Tolofua. The French international hooker had also been under his care after a fusion surgery procedure. In fact, when Jonathan was mapping out Luke's program he was reading largely from Tolofua's previous spreadsheet. We were in good hands! Once the consultant had given Luke the thumbs up, he could begin Jonathan's program. He introduced Luke to a laser pen mounted on a scrum hat. Luke had to adopt a certain position with his chin pushed back, his neck in a neutral position and the idea was that he would manoeuvre the dot on the wall created by the laser pen. This would be done under specific controlled conditions working the smaller muscles on the inside of his neck. He would also work on his range of movement from left to right which at first was limited. There was also a range of exercises using the physio bands which Luke would conduct several times a week. Jonathan also suggested bio-oil which I had never heard of. This was to rub in to his scar in order to smooth it over and blend it in with his natural skin colour. It was fascinating over the months to watch it do just that!

I bought a laser pen on line but sadly it was nowhere as good as the one Jonathan had been using, but it did the trick. I taped it to a cricket cap so that it pointed straight ahead and Luke was then able to begin his exercises. For his range of movement, he began pointing the laser pen into the corner of his bedroom, stood opposite the corner at 45° and we put tape down on the carpet so that he could always adopt exactly the same position. I then used two triangular cards and blue tack to mark the extent of his range as he moved his head from left to right. On each occasion Luke made progress and I was able to move the markers further out. It was an excellent way for him to identify his progress, which was significant. We found various places in the room to tie the physio bands and conduct his exercises and in order to encourage him I did some of them with him. After many months of inactivity, it was wonderful to see Luke exercising and it seemed a very clear first step on a long path back to playing the game he loved so much. It was an exciting time for us all and I recall filming some of his exercises and posting them on the group chat to the fellows back in Mendoza. They were all so excited and full of praise and joy.

It was around that time also, that we received an invitation from Juan Figallo to attend one of Saracens' European clashes. We were going to watch Saracens play Lyon at Allianz Park. Juan had already given Luke a Saracens shirt which was a lovely gesture and once again very much in keeping with rugby culture and tradition, but this was a second thoughtful gesture which again did much to raise Luke's morale and encourage him with his rehab. When we received the tickets there was yet more excitement: these were tickets to the players' lounge! We would be watching the game amongst the players' friends and family. The lounge itself is high up in the stand with a bar and on arrival we were invited to help ourselves from the buffet where delicious food and nibbles were laid out. A lovely surprise that I had not considered was that I bumped into Jane and Ian George. I had not seen them for several years and was delighted to introduce them to Luke. They of course by now had heard of Luke's story and were both sympathetic and encouraging. We sat down to watch the game and I have to say that Saracens very much brought their *A game*. Lyon were dominated in just about every area and it was a convincing victory for the home side. At half-time, Luke and I were able to catch up with Nick Isiekwe who was recovering from an ankle injury. We chatted for a while and again he too was extremely supportive and encouraging with Luke. Nick had not long left Haileybury yet had already achieved international honours and was making a name for himself in the premiership. He is such a lovely chap and on this occasion was generous with his time and comments. I know it was a real treat for Luke. We wished him well for his own recovery and took our seats for the second half. After the game we were able to catch up with Juan and meet his lovely family. Of course we thanked him for this lovely opportunity. Slowly but surely players began to come up for their post-match meal. I must say that the Lyon players seemed pretty glum, but sat by himself at the end of a long table was coach Pierre Mignoni. He looked absolutely livid and was wearing one of those faces that clearly announced to anyone close by that now was not a good time to approach for a chat! When Jamie George came up he was quick to come over and greet us and chat with Luke. That was also a kind gesture as he was rushing off for a night out to celebrate his birthday. I remember thinking a birthday celebration on the back of a massive win against Lyon is likely to be quite something. I'm sure it went well! And so Luke and I said a final goodbye to Juan, Jane and Ian and walked back to our car and set off home. It had been a wonderful experience for us both, but I knew that it had been an excellent boost for Luke. The support he was receiving was now extending far beyond the crucially exceptional levels he had enjoyed in Mendoza.

Barbarians versus Argentina

Luke was now settled in to a routine and to all intents and purposes, other than the lack of any co-curricular activities in school, he was going about his business as normal. In the evenings he would combine doing Jonathan's exercises with homework and some R&R, usually in the form of playing Fifa on his Xbox or watching episodes of The Walking Dead. We had been in contact on and off with the lovely people at the Injured Players Foundation since Luke's injury with Dean Holder frequently asking after Luke's news and checking on his progress. Right at the end of the October half-term we received a very exciting invitation to join the IPF in their executive box at Twickenham to watch the Barbarians take on Argentina on 1st December. I quickly calculated that this was a Saturday during term time. My heart sank for a moment as for us, Saturday is a normal day of school and would either of us be able to attend? I was hopeful that in the circumstances, Luke would be allowed to miss lessons in the morning and I would be able to arrange some cover in the afternoon to run my rugby game. I was sharing a team that season with a new colleague and housemaster, Dougal Lyon. It was a thoroughly enjoyable season despite not having the strongest of teams. The enjoyment was entirely due to the fact that I had such a tremendous coaching partner with a great sense of humour. When I floated the idea of me attending the Barbarians game rather than assisting him on the Saturday afternoon, he had no hesitation in sending me on my way. I had one lesson on the Saturday morning, my fifth form class. Strangely enough Luke was in fact in that class. Yes! I was Luke's French teacher! Given the importance of their GCSE year, I would teach that class and we would set off immediately afterwards. Dean Holder and the folks at the IPF had offered us three tickets so without hesitation I also invited Luke's grandfather. I knew that my dad would really enjoy the occasion and on top of everything else, it was going to be his birthday on the 9th.

Despite the excitement of the prospect of not only watching an international at Twickenham but also enjoying the benefits of watching from an executive box, the busyness of school life meant that for a while, the whole prospect slipped my mind. One day however, I went to my pigeonhole as I do every day and noticed an incredibly smart envelope with very clearly stamped England Rugby branding on it. Good quality card too! I became very excited as I recognised exactly what it was that I was opening. I was giddy like a schoolboy! As I drew forth the contents of this envelope I saw a smartly designed card pouch with the words *executive box* emblazoned in gold writing. Within the card I found the three tickets and a pass for the car park. I'd been attending Twickenham since I was a schoolboy and the concept of driving there and parking had always seemed to me something of an untouchable Holy Grail! I now really couldn't wait.

The Master kindly gave me permission to attend and all we needed to do was to wait patiently for 1st December to come around. During those weeks, Luke continued his routine and I was able to consider what this invitation meant. The more I thought about it the more meaning I added. It became clear to me that on the day, there would potentially be a number of former players in wheelchairs. I discussed this with my wife and with Luke, questioning what effect the sight of these players might have. At the time, Luke was very much in the early stages of his rehab program that would last right through to the following August at which point he would engage in a steady program of returning to contact before the start of the 2019/20 season. Would the sight of these chaps sow the seed of second thoughts for Luke? And how would it affect me? From the start, I had been relieved to hear that once Luke had been fixed, there ought to be no reason why he shouldn't return to playing rugby, yet I would be faced with the sight of what I considered to be absolutely the reason why he shouldn't return to rugby. The worst-case scenario would be another fracture, this time causing some level of paralysis. Then the words of the medical director of the UAR rang in my ears: the risk will be no greater than anyone else taking the field. There is such a great deal at stake. Haileybury was no stranger to such incidents. In the 1960s a well-known player called Danny Hearn had become paralysed during a brutal collision while playing against the All Blacks. Mr Hearn had been a teacher at Haileybury, in fact he was still there when I joined the school in 1999.

Famously, he coached the school's 1st XV for many years, from his wheelchair. He is quite a well-known figure and certainly familiar to the IPF and the tackle itself is even on Youtube! More recently, Mark Bowen a front row forward in Haileybury's 1st XV pack had been paralysed during a collapsed scrum.

The more I thought about it all, the more terrible and terrifying it became. Of course the reality dawned heavily on me that the very reason we were given passes to the car park was that some of the IPF guests on the day will have needed to park close by as a matter of imperative practicality and for a while at least, I had been considering it a treat. Thoughtless! The IPF were doing such sterling work and had been for a long time that it became clear to me I should consider the whole exercise with a good deal more positivity and purpose. This was a fantastic organisation reaching out to Luke as something of a success story; a good news story. He had been broken and he had been fixed. The likelihood was that he would play again and this was seen as very positive and uplifting. Luke seemed to have none of my worries and ploughed on as he had been throughout the whole experience thus far. If he did have concerns, he was keeping them to himself.

The drive there was uneventful, thank goodness, and armed with my pass, I was guided to our parking spot not 50 yards from the stadium. We had been invited to arrive extremely early, around three hours before kick-off and thus the car park itself was pretty much empty and staff were going this way and that preparing their various stands for the big event. Stewards politely showed us the way to our box and on arrival we were greeted by a charming lady called Caroline who worked for the IPF. Immediately, we were introduced to the other guests that had already arrived. There was a lovely feel to the atmosphere which was warm and friendly. There were two gentlemen in wheelchairs, one I would say in his 40s and one in his 50s both accompanied by friends or family. We were invited to have a coffee or cup of tea and were given our match programmes. The room itself was stylishly decorated and comfortably furnished with chairs and tables upon which later we would have our lunch. We wandered out through the sliding glass doors into the vast echoing openness of the hollow stadium to our front. The place was completely empty apart from stewards in their hi-vis vests conducting various tasks including the fascinating sight of what looked like a security sweep around all the tiers. We speculated that they were either checking that every seat in the stadium was fully functional or checking for suspicious packages. Possibly both. At ground level, a large number of television staff were laying what seemed to be miles and miles of cables this way and that such that certain corners look like giant plates of black shiny spaghetti. Cameramen were positioning their equipment and the grounds team were putting the final touches to what once again looked like a magnificent playing surface.

We had been told that one of the highlights of the day would be an opportunity to meet the head groundsman down by the pitch. Now at this point I must confess to being something of a lawn enthusiast/geek! I spend a lot of time going up and down in various directions with a petrol driven cylinder mower trying to fashion the best possible surface. With limited means, time and equipment I manage okay and certainly do well enough to bring a smile to my face from time to time. I was absolutely fascinated and really excited to hear from the man who at his fingertips could boast almost limitless means, time and equipment to produce time after time one of the best playing surfaces around. He did not disappoint at all. Keith Kent was not only a very approachable and kind man, but did an absolutely fantastic job holding all our attention for 20 or so minutes as he went into the finer details of how he and his team prepared the Twickenham surface. My father, Luke and me, along with the other guests had been escorted down to pitch level and were able to wander onto the Astro surface which runs adjacent to the touchline; therefore we were just a few feet away from the hallowed turf. From there we waited a short while and on his arrival Keith greeted us with a beaming smile and an almost childlike enthusiasm. He charmed us all with amusing anecdotes and had a great way with words. I was also riveted by everything he had to say in terms of the technical approach to the grass growing; boring to some I guess, but it really gripped me. He explained that the turf was only 3% synthetic including 200mm nylon threads which poked up sufficiently high to add strength and resilience to the grass covering but not so much that it would get clipped by the mowers. Some might be interested to read that in order to improve the drainage across the ground normal sharp sand is never employed. Such sand is angular and triangular in shape and therefore when it compacts it closes in leaving no space between the particles. Keith spoke highly of the *round sand* which he spreads on the field. The round particles, when compacted still allow space in between thus allowing the soil to drain. It made perfect sense. On the other hand, he was able to offer me little help when it came to dealing with my worm cast problem other than the fact that eventually the worms would do a tremendous job for me spreading what sand I had put down throughout the top layer of soil. I was also interested to hear that a large part of his job involves visiting clubs up and down the country working as a consultant and advising them on the best way to take their facilities to the next level. I can imagine him visiting clubs and his enthusiasm rubbing off on others. I really think it's a job you have to love.

After taking a few photographs pitchside we were then escorted back up to the box for lunch. The IPF team had laid on a wonderful spread and the caterers had really done us proud. Having spent some time in Argentina, I immediately identified the trays of empanadas. I guess that was the caterers' way of paying gastronomic homage to the visiting team that day. They were absolutely delicious and I'd go as far as to say on a par with those we had that day up at the zip lining centre. There was an array of cold meats, salmon, salads, bread and cheese. It really was quite fantastic and we were encouraged by our hosts to dig in and make the very most of it. Some were also making the most of the free beer and wine. It was a nice opportunity to sit round the table and chat with those other guests in the box. They were interested to hear Luke's story and extremely enthusiastic and positive about his prospects of playing again. We sensed a good deal of warmth and encouragement. There was an excellent, friendly atmosphere that permeated throughout the box all day. Shortly before kick-off we went outside and took our seats. As one would expect, there was a terrific atmosphere in the ground and everyone was excited at the prospect of watching the Barbarians. The Barbarians had picked a thrilling and very international line-up with a large number of top South African performers. There was a huge amount of skill on show from both teams and with under a minute to go the scores were level at 35 – 35. I sat in my seat thinking what a great way for such a game to end, the honours even, the crowd thoroughly entertained and there would be no loser. Each executive box has a flatscreen suspended from the roof of the tier above, facing directly inwards so that people can watch replays and other graphics. I took a photograph of the level scores on the screen in order to send it to our buddies in Mendoza. As I was replacing my phone in a pocket, the Barbarians made some ground into the Argentinian half and out of nowhere the fly half dropped a goal from 35m out to claim victory. It was an amazing piece of skill and I don't hold it against the player at all, however, from our point of view, I know Luke and I would have preferred Argentina to win or for the scores to have remained level. Both teams had played with real ambition and a clear intent to entertain. Neither deserved to lose.

On the day I had been extremely proud to wear the Los Tordos RC shirt that young Gonzalo had given Luke back in the *Clinica Francesa*. Sadly, it is not at all a good fit for Luke and even a little tight for his father! Middle-aged spread has taken hold and tight fitting modern rugby shirts are not ideal. Where does that *back fat* come from? Men in their early to mid-forties will know exactly what I'm talking about: that area just below one's kidneys that has always been very firm, suddenly and without warning doubles in size and wobbles about like a supermarket own brand crème caramel. Anyhow, I squeezed into this shirt and managed to keep it on, in relative comfort, for the whole day. After the game, we were invited once more to make the most of the tea, coffee and cakes or indeed to polish off the lunch. Nobody seemed in any great rush to leave and it was nice to talk to people about their lives and to learn more about the foundation, an organisation that offered support of all kinds, financial and otherwise, to players with serious injuries.

We'd had a lovely day and on our way back to the car we noticed that the Argentinian players had now showered, had a meal and were boarding their team bus prior to departure.

There was a handful of Argentinian fans crowded around and a few were chatting to players as they went past. Luke had hoped to grab a word with Tomi Cubelli before he boarded the bus and we waited patiently. It was clear on the face of most of the players that they were absolutely livid to have lost and particularly in the last seconds of the game. Player after player came out and boarded the bus and while some stopped for brief chats, autographs and selfies it was abundantly clear that their hearts were not really in it. When Tomi finally walked out of the stadium towards the bus he had a face like a storm and Luke, I feel quite rightly, decided not to call out for his attention and just allowed him to walk past, board the bus and take a seat allowing him some time to reflect. I felt that was the correct decision of Luke's, which displayed a good deal of maturity, respect for the player and just emotional intelligence beyond his years. I was a little disappointed for him, but proud too of his actions and we had enjoyed an absolutely fabulous and memorable day in any case. Apart from anything else, it was a great opportunity to spend some quality time with my father and in that respect, it was simply a really enjoyable boys' day out.

Saracens Support

One day in Dining Hall, I was sat having lunch with colleagues when I was introduced to a new member of staff working in the Development Office. As it happened, our new colleague turned out to be the wife of Saracens and Scotland legend, Kelly Brown. Emily and I spoke on many occasions about Luke, his injury and subsequent program of rehabilitation and indeed on one occasion she said that Kelly had heard about Luke. She showed a huge amount of care and interest and suggested that if ever I wished to take Luke to Allianz Park, that she felt Kelly would be able to assist with tickets. For the sake of inspiring Luke, I thought this was a great idea and remembered how excited he had been to watch Saracens demolish Lyon earlier in the European campaign.

Not long afterwards Emily asked if we were able to go to the European clash against Glasgow. As luck would have it, it was the first day of the Easter holiday and a great way to begin our break. We had been given instructions to go and collect our tickets from the office and on the day were kindly allowed to use one of the car parks. It was a quarter-final and there was a phenomenal atmosphere in the ground. This was helped by one of the warmest days so far in the year and just for once it didn't seem to be a blowing a howling wind through Allianz Park. As we queued to pick up the tickets we bumped into Juan Figallo who was delighted to see Luke and asked after his progress. Evidently, he was still injured himself.

On receipt of our tickets we noticed that they were standing room only so headed pitch-side to identify a good spot. Fortunately, we were there in good time and were able to secure a spot right up against the barrier in the corner of the pitch looking straight down the inside of the touchline. We congratulated ourselves on finding a good spot and enjoyed the rest of the warm-up. On the day, Saracens were very much in the mood and recorded a memorable victory over the Glaswegians.

Things did not start well for Saracens, however, and the visitors scored an excellent try from a line-out on the halfway line. Twice a decoy runner was used in the midfield after clean ball *off the top* and the inclusion of the blindside wing added the extra man allowing the very strong Rory Hughes room on the outside. He eventually put in a deft pass back inside to the ever willing support runner, Ali Price. He raced across the line right in front of us. There was less than two minutes on the clock. The Saracens reply was almost instant with a delicate chip over the top destined to land in the Glasgow in-goal area. Welsh full-back Liam Williams was the chaser and rose above the defenders to claim the ball and score right between the posts. It was followed shortly afterwards with a now rampant Saracens claiming a try on the right wing via David Strettle after a number of phases and deft handling, including one contribution from Old

Haileyburian Jamie George, who had filled in at scrum-half at the final breakdown. It would be the first of many decisive actions by the England hooker. By now, Saracens were really expressing themselves and after some direct running, clinical ball retention and accurate well-timed passing, including yet another intervention from Jamie George, Captain Brad Barritt scored down the left-hand side. Early in the second half there was another try from Liam Williams, this time taking a crash ball off a ruck set up by Jamie George five metres out after the hooker had found himself on the wing. In agonising circumstances for the Glasgow team, David Strettle then rather too easily picked off an interception on the halfway line to sprint in under the posts. After a ruthless catch and drive from another accurate line-out throw in, Jamie George scored in our corner, which of course was a great delight for us. The flow was temporarily reversed with a wonderful score for Glasgow down the right-hand side with the ball flowing through multiple hands before George Horne went over for the five pointer. By now though, the score was already 49-20 with 10 minutes to go so the outlook was bleak for the visitors. The home side, however, was not done and after a strong carry from another Old Haileyburian, Nick Isiekwe, the ball was shipped to the impressive young centre Nick Tompkins who bundled over under the posts. There was one last try for Glasgow in the dying seconds bringing the final score to 56-27. It was a thrilling and thoroughly entertaining game which Luke and I really relished, but to cap it all, Jamie George was (quite rightly) named man of the match. I texted a photo of Luke and me at the ground to Emily, with a big thank you.

Having watched two rounds of the European competition, when Saracens made it to the English Premiership final, I didn't hesitate to buy tickets to take Luke along to Twickenham. What a memorable game that was! Exeter looked comfortable and were strong during the first half, at one point leading Saracens 27-16, but re-energised in the second half with great individual performances, most notably from the stand-out Maro Itoje, Saracens pulled away and showed their class. Jamie George put the finishing touch on a spectacular comeback with a try between the posts bringing the score to 27-37. Exeter were to score again in the dying moments of the match but it was not enough to stop Saracens claiming their fifth premiership championship.

The game as an exercise in sporting theatre was hugely memorable; I may perhaps remember the day however for other reasons. On taking our seats high up in the upper tier on about halfway, I spotted a group of Exeter fans sat to our left in the same row. Three seats along was a chap that I thought looked identical to someone I had been at school with and had not seen for about 30 years. I leaned over and asked the supporter nearest to us, "Excuse me, is your friend there called Nick?" "Yes," he replied. "Nick Loader?" I asked. "Yes," was the response. "Crikey, I used to go to school with him!" Eventually, with a bit of seat swapping, Nick and I watched the game sat side-by-side reminiscing about school life and of course giving each other the obligatory, and *semi-expert* commentary on the game as it unfolded. It was a splendid surprise and I could not believe that in a ground holding 82,000 spectators, I should be placed three seats away from an old school friend. I guess these things happen.

Luke and I had really appreciated experiencing Saracens' success together, taking great joy in every moment of excitement. Having teenage boys is not all fun and games. There are long periods of time apart, when the young man in question is locked away in his room playing various games and speaking with great enthusiasm to friends over various technical wizardry platforms which leave me utterly bamboozled. On entering the bedroom, one is almost always greeted with silence or the occasional grunt which after some consideration and careful deciphering is able to be understood, though the aid of context is usually essential. So for me, it was a real treat to spend quality time with Luke in an environment we were both fanatical about. In many respects I can certainly claim that our relationship was enriched by Luke's injury and the many opportunities to interact and engage with each other that followed.

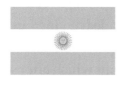 

Sunday 14th April – a first return to rugby

Luke had played mini rugby at Hertford RFC since he was five. Hertford is a great club and only 2.5 miles from our home so it has very much been part of our lives since moving to the area. I started playing there back in 1999 and have continued on and off, work permitting, to play ever since. Now I occasionally turn out for the vets alongside old chums from younger, more flexible and pacier times! I have also assisted with the coaching of Luke's year group and have always refereed their matches if at all possible. Darron Moore, the lead coach for Luke's club team was one of the first people I contacted with news of Luke's injury from Argentina. His heart-warming messages were a source of reassurance and encouragement during those difficult and anxious early days. Since our return to the UK, I returned a few times to assist with training sessions and on each occasion the coaches and players showed great interest, sympathy and support.

I remember very distinctly the first time I came along, Darron stopped the session and brought over the boys so that I could address them all to give them an update on how Luke was getting on. They stood, as rugby players tend to, instinctively creating a circle around the coach and listened attentively. Back on the touchline, a few parents were congregated and of course were full of sympathy and questions. Many were surprised to hear that Luke was set on a path that would eventually culminate in a return to playing rugby and I lost count of the number of times I heard the question "How does his mother feel about that?" On most occasions, my reply would be "not very enthusiastic!" Personally, I have hugely mixed feelings about his return. I'm writing parts of this book very much as it all unfolds and I do find myself at times questioning why I am being so supportive of his return to rugby. I know it is his passion and I know how much it has brought me over the years and I keep hearing about players who have had fusion surgery and continue to play. I also have the words of the medical director in Argentina ringing in my ears telling me that the risk of him doing it again would be "the same as any other player taking the field". And so with Luke deciding he wishes to return to rugby, the only thing to do is to support that decision wholeheartedly and to do everything I can to ensure that when he does, that it is in the safest possible conditions. Therefore, we have routinely returned to see Jonathan George whenever necessary and I've supported Luke at the gym and at home with his various exercises.

With our youngest revising for GCSE's and recovering from a serious injury and our oldest off to university in Durham, family time when we are the four of us is at a premium. One Saturday in April, we found ourselves going to the cinema to watch the latest superhero film on 4DX. I must say if you haven't tried 4DX, it's an extraordinary cinema experience! Just before the main feature started, I withdrew my phone to switch it off and noticed a text from Darron. "Mate, just had ref cry off with broken toe. Don't suppose you could fill in tomorrow, 11am KO?" I was happy to oblige as I really enjoyed our outing on the Hertford first-team pitch the previous week when our U16 team had had a good game and ran out winners. Despite feeling extraordinarily stiff for several days afterwards (I don't do much exercise these days), I was happy to return the following Sunday to referee another game. I had spoken with Luke and asked him if he would like to come along with me and act as one of the touch judges. It would be his first sort of return to rugby and certainly the first time he had been back to the club and seen his teammates and coaches since the previous season. His last game for the club had been the U15 County Cup Final against Bishop's Stortford, held at Old Albanians RFC, a losing encounter the previous spring. He was very excited about the prospect of simply getting involved.

On this occasion, with an 11:30am KO, we arrived at approximately 10:50am and strolled over to the pitch. As we drew nearer, several parents and a couple of coaches were on the touchline by a sea of kit spread in all directions. They were delighted to see Luke with handshakes all round and encouraging remarks about how well he was looking. As I wandered onto the field to greet Darron he decided to interrupt the warm-up and brought the squad over to us. Once again the boys set themselves up in a circle around Darron who gave a brief but extremely heartfelt and warm speech, explaining how fantastic it was to see Luke on his feet, back at the club and looking so well. In what was a wonderful gesture before returning to their warm-up, the boys instinctively started clapping, as is often the case and traditional, as a mark of respect for an injured player. That Luke was now returning, even in this small way was also worthy of note and of a quick round of applause. I found the whole process very moving and a huge feeling of pride for my son bubbled to the surface.

After the game, Luke and I sat at the bar for a good while chatting to some parents who again were very encouraging and interested to hear Luke's progress. I think the experience did a lot to encourage Luke to work hard and look forward even more to returning to playing. This goal was of course still many, many months away!

A few days later, we had another session with Jonathan George at Saracens training centre at Old Albanians RFC. On this occasion, as we walked into the physio area, Saracens captain Brad Barritt was receiving some attention on one of the various physio benches. We walked through to a room and Jonathan asked a number of questions to gauge how Luke was progressing. He explained during this session that Luke would be testing his neck strength to assess his progress and give him a platform of data from which he could monitor further improvements with a view to a final assessment as to whether Luke would be safe to return to playing rugby. It was a useful reminder at the time, that a return to rugby was not a simple inevitability and that decisions would have to be made along the way. It was a subtle wake-up call. Jonathan began by explaining to Luke how the process would work and showed him a range of spreadsheets from archive documents explaining the kind of result he would be looking for. We then made our way over to the Saracens gym where, after a short warm-up, Luke was strapped in to some kind of pressure gauge. He would test his neck's strength in the four directions he had been working on in such determined fashion: extension, flexion, left flexion and right flexion. The results were pleasing and Jonathan was at pains to explain that the ratio between the results was the key information. Flexion was always expected to be weaker than extension and is the case for almost everybody who does this kind of exercise but the expected figure was around 66% of extension. On this occasion Luke's flexion was more like 46% so at the end of the session, Jonathan sat me down and reshaped his weekly routine to bias the work on his flexion in order to redress the imbalance. I remember Jonathan as a schoolboy and his twin brother Gareth and he had helped our family move house. It is such a joy to see him now settled in work that he loves and that he is extremely good at. We walked away with a clear idea of how to go about the next month and half or so and agreed to meet again in June. We also discussed the possibility of Luke working with Haileybury's strength and conditioning coach, Joe Satt, who had been on the tour to South America with us. Jonathan knows Joe well and simply suggested that Joe got in touch to discuss how best Luke could make use of the weights room and Joe's experience.

Thank You to Los Tordos

Right from the word go, it was clear that our school should make some kind of gesture of thanks to the folks at Los Tordos Rugby Club. After all, Luke's injury had taken place during a school trip and the club had not only gone out of their way to look after one of the school's charges but also a member of staff. He had been not only conducting his fatherly duties, but also executing his job as a member of staff with official and professional obligations. Many thoughts had crossed my mind over the months such as sending signed shirts or other such memorabilia relating to the school that might hang in the clubhouse in Mendoza. In the end, such was the effect on Luke and his growth as a person that I began to consider another option that might equally influence the development of a young Argentinian.

I approached the Master of Haileybury, Martin Collier with a proposal. I suggested inviting a promising young rugby player whose English was sufficiently good to not only survive but thrive at our school to spend the first term of the Lower Sixth with us as our guest, boarding and learning as a pupil at Haileybury. It would be a personal privilege and pleasure of mine as a housemaster, to welcome this young Mendocino to my own boarding house, Lawrence. It then occurred to me, that LTRC was a girls' Hockey club too and during our first term of the year, our girls play hockey and that we should extend the invitation to one of their girls.

Mr Collier was a big fan of this suggestion and immediately endorsed it with enthusiasm suggesting that we might also offer to pay for their flights. He was certainly adamant that an issue of finance should not be a showstopper in allowing this gesture of goodwill on our part to come to fruition.

I immediately contacted my friends in Mendoza to communicate our offer and the news was received with genuine appreciation and no small amount of excitement. I had explained the simple parameters that we were looking for a competent rugby player and hockey player and that both should have a reasonable level of English. I remembered from my time visiting the club, that there was a big range of abilities when it came to speaking English. It became very clear that at their end, this opportunity for two of their young players to broaden their horizons both culturally and educationally was taken very seriously. An information evening was organised at their clubhouse and applications were invited via a big online launch. Glossy adverts had been designed and created with images of our school. I remember being extremely impressed. So eventually there had been a number of applications. From what I could see following on the Facebook pages of this wonderful club, there were a few shortlisted and eventually two were selected. From now on, the planning process on how to bring this project into fruition would begin, involving communication between our admissions department and the families directly. For a few years the school had been working in association with other schools around the world giving opportunities for talented sportsman and women, on an exchange basis, to enjoy the benefits and cultures of studying in different countries. This arrangement was different, however. This was not an exchange; this was a thank you. Several months down the line I was at a meeting with all the housemasters, housemistresses and senior leaders discussing the state of our prospects for the following year in terms of pupil numbers. On a screen, at the end of the room was projected the details of the various exchanges that had been planned for the 2019-2020 academic year. I became very excited to see the two slots for the Argentinians. As yet no names or details had been entered, but I sat in my seat, reassured that what had started as a nice idea was now being realised. Exchange pupils and guests - as would be the case in this story - do take up a boarding place and as such is a potential financial loss to the school. That would certainly be the Bursar's point of view. Of course there is some truth in that.

During this particular meeting one of my colleagues posed the question "What is the point of these exchange pupils? Are they really worth it?" The Master began his reply and spoke in detail and enthusiastically about what such exchange pupils brought to us as a school and of course the huge benefits to our boys and girls who would go across the world enjoying the reciprocal arrangement that was in place. He discussed each case one at a time and when it came to the

Argentinians, he glanced over to me and asked if I would like to say a few words by means of an explanation. I had not been ready to speak but was happy enough to share my thoughts on the subject. Many of the people in the room knew Luke's story; however, I began to explain about the incredible support we had received during an almost impossible scenario and as I spoke, despite the fact that many, many months had passed, I became very emotional. Some of the details and particularly some of the information about the individuals involved were such that I began to feel my voice wobbling. Before not too long, I was overwhelmed emotionally as the memories of my 15 year old son and his precarious position on the brink of paralysis came flooding back. My face contorted and tears began rolling down my cheeks. I had long since given up any hope of continuing to address my colleagues and my boss simply had to take over from where I had left off. As I got to grips with myself and the tears subsided, I realised that I had not heard or taken on board any of the words that Mr Collier had said. However, I do remember his last line: "So yes…they are worth it!"

I approached him and apologised for allowing my emotions to get the better of me. I had really thought that after so many months, I would be able to speak about the situation without any problems. Evidently I was wrong! I bumped into the school doctor a few days later who had been at the meeting. I felt it necessary to apologise. On that occasion, she urged me not to worry and simply said, "It shows you are human."

What was important, however, in the long run, was that this plan was destined to go ahead and we would be welcoming two promising Argentinians to our community. I wondered then, how wonderful it would be if Luke's story might conclude with him returning to playing rugby alongside the young man from Mendoza. Eventually, we learnt the names of the selected pair: Manuel, known to us as Manu and Santina, who we would call Santi. Months of email exchanges and paperwork all organised by our registry team came and went and with just two days to go before their arrival I double checked that all was good at their end. I was expecting their arrival at the ungodly hour of 4am, Sunday, 1 September. Strangely enough, this was exactly a year later to the day, that Luke and I returned from Mendoza after the whole ordeal. I had organised for my good buddy Dave Phillips who runs his own taxi firm to pick them up from Gatwick and bring them straight up to us. Dave does a lot of pick-ups for a number of overseas boarders in Lawrence House and has done for some time. I knew him to be totally reliable and had in the past entrusted him with my own children for drop-offs at various airports so I knew they would be in good hands. Alarmingly though, Dolores, Manu's mother kept referring to the arrival on Saturday. Eventually after some investigating I found out that a colleague from the registry team had been flummoxed by the +1 day appearance on the tickets and told me they were arriving on the 1st at 0400! In fact, they were arriving the day before at the same time. So our two new friends would spend two days with us as a family before the term was officially to start and good old Dave (who if you remember, bumped into us at Heathrow Arrivals, the day we returned with Penny) was happy to change his plans at short notice. All's well that ends well, I guess!

It turned out to be a really nice opportunity to get to know them as people and add our own more personal touch to the gesture of thanks that the school was offering. The two days went very quickly and it was nice family time. Manu and Luke very quickly bonded and it was a good opportunity for Manu and Santi to get a feel for their surroundings before the madness and organised chaos of the start of a new academic year!

They did not arrive empty-handed: Manu and Santi had offered wine of course, but they also produced a plaque that had been made. This was a large brass plaque with Haileybury's logo and the crest of Los Tordos Rugby Club. The plaque itself was mounted on a thick, heavy piece of wood and the whole thing was rather splendid. The inscription too was very meaningful: *"From Los Tordos RC of Argentina to Haileybury, in gratitude for their generosity and their strong commitment to the training of young people."*

Manu also went into his suitcase and took out a gift that he had carried all the way from Argentina on Juan's behalf. This was a personal gift from Juan to me. He handed over a cream linen bag about a foot long with a string tie at one end, closing off the contents. I was intrigued as to what was inside. As I loosened the tie and reached inside my hands clearly identified the handle of a knife. As I pulled it out, I instantly drew a breath of surprise. It was a beautiful piece of craftsmanship. The handle of this knife had chrome features at either end and a beautifully crafted fabric handle with South American styling. Huge skill had clearly gone in to its production. I drew the blade from its thick leather sheath. It was a 14 cm long carving blade or perhaps steak knife. It was a stunningly beautiful piece and as I turned it over I noted that Juan had had my full name inscribed on the blade and underneath my name, I could read his initials. It was a beautifully touching and personal gift from one man to another. I immediately contacted him on WhatsApp in order to thank him for such a "special gift". His reply was simple and to the point: "it's a special present for a special person." I remember thinking that of all the people in this story such as the surgeons, our new friends in Mendoza who had supported us, the Pumas, Jonathan George, Juan Figallo and so many more and of course Luke himself, I was the <u>least special</u>! These guys were all going out of their way to provide invaluable yet unconditional assistance. I was simply being Luke's dad. However, Juan's present in itself made me feel special.

As for our two guests, within the first fortnight of the term, Santi had been selected to play for the girls' 1st XI and indeed represented the college at the Olympic Park in a victory against Epsom College and Manu after one game in the 2nd XV, traditionally called the XXX, was moved up to the 1st XV. Manu also settled in to life as a boarder with great ease, quickly picking up the sense of house spirit and in brief was a real hit with the boys. He studied hard with the new subjects that he had been given and on his first report one of his teachers quite rightly used the words: "he is a credit to his club and his country." As ambassadors for their club, Santi and Manu did a fantastic job making the most of the opportunity that they had been offered, making it possible in the future, to consider repeating this exercise. Friends and family at LTRC, with the help of various social media platforms such as Instagram and Facebook, have continued to show interest and support for this venture and relationship.

Rehab – the long road

It has been a real privilege to have been able to take Luke along to Jonathan George at Saracens. He has closely monitored Luke's progress and continues to show great interest and offer support and encouragement. That Jonathan had such knowledge and experience conducting the same kind of rehabilitation on two professionals and internationals of the game was a constant source of reassurance and indeed inspiration for Luke.

It will come as no surprise that the immediate order of the day from the Argentine surgeon was total rest. This of course was backed up by the consultant in the UK when we returned. The path that was laid out by Mr Ahmed was very clear and Jonathan began to plan Luke's long-term schedule around that guidance. Luke took no part in any activity until October, two months after his injury. This was a source of real frustration and low moments. On 16th of October, Luke had the green light to start his rehab. At this point he was only allowed some short sessions on the cycling machine which at first Luke found quite difficult. However, he worked hard and adhered to the only stipulation, that he should maintain a neutral head position throughout. The opportunity to run was still some way away at this point. The zero impact nature of cycling was the perfect place to kick off. Luke of course is extremely lucky in that he lives on the campus at school and the well-equipped fitness suite is just a short walk away. In addition, the school introduced a rehab period on a Tuesday and Thursday afternoon when the rest of the school, essentially the fit and able, are having their sport and games sessions. It is therefore supervised and guided which again is a great help and a source of reassurance that not only the exercises are done but they are done correctly.

Early in November we met with Jonathan and he introduced some of the exercises that he had previously conducted with Chris Tolofua and Juan Figallo. These were exercises involving the laser pen I mentioned earlier, under strict control, using the smaller internal muscles around the neck to manoeuvre the dot. This was something new and exciting and Luke bought into it with real enthusiasm. There were other exercises such as manoeuvring the dot through a Union Jack style pattern on the wall created by tape, where the dot had to continually pass through the centre. Another was starting with the dot in the centre of the tape, moving his head over to the right or left, closing his eyes and then attempting to bring the dot back to the centre. Luke really enjoyed that challenge.

He was also encouraged to do some basic physical upper body work using some physio's bands. These elastic bands were hard work and he was given a range of exercises which he duly executed. On one occasion I filmed him and sent it to the group chat and as usual there were many replies of encouragement and cheer. We had also been instructed to purchase one of those sleeves you strap to your arm in order to measure one's blood pressure. We were given specific instructions to inflate the armband to a certain pressure and Luke was told to lay flat on his back with the inflated band under his head. Adopting the position he had been using throughout, that is to say chin back and head in a neutral position, he had to push down on the inflated band, now serving as a pressure pad under his head. He would push down under control, holding a certain pressure reading on the gauge for a number of seconds and a set number of reps. I was impressed with Luke's discipline particularly with regards to the technical side of what he was trying to achieve.

A month passed, with Luke spending the evenings in his bedroom working with the laser pen, the band-work and the holds, before progressing to the next stage. Once again we met with Jonathan and on this occasion he took us over to the gym where the Saracens squads work out. It was an exciting and interesting place to be. I recall one of the first things I noticed as I walked in was a collection of trainers on the left-hand side just within the gym. There was a giant pair of bright yellow trainers standing out from the crowd. I had never seen shoes quite this size. I had to ask Jonathan who on earth they belonged to and he replied Will Skelton. Of course it came as no surprise as the man has a giant frame and nature had quite sensibly provided the necessary structural support at the end of his legs. Apparently they were size 18!

We moved across to one of the machines where Jonathan set up a bench and invited Luke to sit down. He introduced us for the first time to a head harness that would be connected to the weights machine. Luke would begin a process of *neck loading* by which he would sit bolt upright, with the harness strapped across his head and physically hold the weights with the strength of his neck. This was quite an alarming sight for a parent but the weights were light, Luke was being expertly guided and I knew that this was the first step to ensuring that he would have a strong enough neck to return to playing rugby the following season. All that seemed a long way away and we were only taking the first small steps. Once again Luke had to ensure that his head was in a neutral position, that his chin was tucked in and that his shoulders were back. This would be the position he would have to get used to for all his exercises. He would now begin a program of endurance meaning he would have a lighter weight but longer holds. He began with 30 second holds and then over the course of a couple of months would move to 45, 60, then 90 seconds. Luke was doing four sets of these holds, with an equally long break in between each hold and would do this in all four directions. We had purchased our own harness after Jonathan had convinced us that it would be the best investment we would make. He wasn't wrong! The harness would be strapped first across his forehead then the back of his head then his left and right sides. It was never very comfortable to watch, although I confess of course it was far more hard work to complete the exercises. Luke showed a good deal of determination during this phase.

It was during this period of endurance neck loading that Luke was first permitted to begin running. This needed to be conducted at a slow and steady pace and in a straight line. So almost in the most literal sense, this was another step in the right direction. He made full use of course of the running machines in the school gym and it was great to add a little variety to his routine. Once again he took to his task steadfastly. After a brief exchange on WhatsApp with Jonathan, it was agreed that since he was running now, it would also be appropriate for him to start a program of lower body work on the available machines at school. Once again the only stipulation from Jonathan was that Luke was disciplined about keeping a straight back and particularly a neutral head position. On the occasions when I was with Luke in the gym, I tried to remind him if he was falling short on a technical area. Despite the fact that I was doing my very best, it was not uncommon for Luke to snap at me. I guess it could have been because he was working hard and in some discomfort and perhaps I had timed my instructions poorly, but at the same time Luke had a tendency to not recognise that all I was doing was attempting to be supportive.

Luke's return to running was not without incident and given he had not run since the previous August he had some issues with his Achilles. Jonathan was very reassuring and immediately identified it, suggesting that it would be easy to fix and so it would turn out. A couple of weeks of the exercises that he had suggested solved the problem almost immediately. Around February it was time for Luke to move on to the upper body work. By now he had done a number of months of endurance neck loading and Jonathan was satisfied that he could move on. Jonathan was kind enough to come over to Haileybury and to join Luke for his first session up in the gym working the upper body. This was also an opportunity, as I was not around, for Jonathan to meet with Celeste and give her an idea of Luke's progress and reassure her of a likely successful outcome. The Haileybury gym is well equipped and Luke was able to set about working on a range of upper body machines. It was at this time too, that the Saracens physio switched Luke over from endurance work to strength work with his neck loading. From now the length of the holds would be reduced but the weight would be increased. He came down from 90 second holds to 20 seconds and the weight almost doubled.

In February, he saw the consultant at the Princess Alexandra Hospital, who, after examining the x-ray that we had taken that day, announced that the metalwork fixations that had been put in by Mr Terraza were still firmly in place and that new bone was beginning to grow, announcing therefore that the fusion process had begun. This was reassuring and he went on to say that after a further three months, Luke could consider returning to some contact sport. Luke of course was delighted, although the prospect of another three months to wait was not received with much relish. However, we had known from the very start that this would be a long and patient process. Everyone had told us the same thing and it was highlighted by the international rugby players who visited Luke in hospital. Patience would be the key! During those months of waiting, Luke continued with his program occasionally deciding to raise the weight of his holds. He also saw Jonathan at one point a little further down the line in order to test his neck strength. As described earlier, his ratio flexion / extension was below what we had hoped and therefore Jonathan decided to tweak his program so that he was doing more work on his weaker side. The flexion is always weaker than extension but the ratio should be more like 3/5. Luke was short on that and therefore that was his target during the next few months.

1st May was the big day that had been agreed with the consultant. He could return to some more sporty activities such as kicking a ball around with his buddies on the Astro, taking part in touch rugby and anything else that might take his fancy. I recall heading to the gym with him for his usual program but beginning to take a ball with us so that afterwards we could hop onto the Astro and have a kick around. It was such a joy to see Luke running around with a rugby ball. It is difficult to adequately describe how excited Luke appeared. He had an extraordinary boost of energy and would run around chasing after balls like he did as a toddler. He showed a seemingly bottomless pit of energy and enthusiasm. All this he did with a huge grin on his face. It was quite wonderful to watch. This period also coincided with the beginning of the summer rugby program organised by Michael Owen. He would run weekly sessions of small-sided games on Terrace. These looked incredibly tough physically and it was phenomenally exciting to see Luke back in action and working so hard. It was clear that he would make the most of every second of each game. I decided to take a video clip of one of the sessions in order to post it to our friends in Mendoza. I got lucky on the first take as having approached the touchline and raised my phone, Luke was immediately in action. Playing down the left-hand side during a conditioned game of touch in which one player from your team was allowed to stand anywhere in front of the ball, Luke received a pass from teammate Callum McGurk. Luke held up the defender as Callum wrapped around on a loop and Luke found him with a pass out of the backdoor as Callum made a run down the left wing. Callum fixed the cover defence and found Luke on the inside with a flip pass which allowed Luke to open his legs for a bit of a gallop. By now the offside player in his team had taken the direct route to the try line and Luke found him with a 15 metre spin pass off his left hand. I couldn't believe how lucky I was that I wouldn't have to spend another half an hour trying to catch some action on my phone and the icing on the cake was provided by the booming voice of Michael Owen that echoed around Terrace; "Oh that's magic, Luke!" I posted the video without hesitation. Our friends in Mendoza were really excited to see Luke not only running but taking part in our game of rugby, albeit touch and making good contributions. I walked home very satisfied and happy that day.

July saw the prospect of beginning a program of strength and conditioning with the guidance of Haileybury's strength and conditioning coach, Joe Satt. Joe of course had been on the tour to South America and so perhaps had even more interest in Luke's progress than might ordinarily have been the case. Joe, who was good friends with Jonathan George, liaised with the Saracens physio to come up with a suitable plan and program for Luke. Before setting off for his summer holiday, Joe met with Luke and me in the school's well equipped weights room to go step-by-step through each exercise. It was a complex program involving three sessions, upper body, lower body and total body. There were several exercises involved in each session and the number of reps and sets clearly laid out in a spreadsheet. Joe had done a very precise and clear job. We were there at least an hour going through each exercise and Joe was meticulous in pointing out the technical necessities for each one. It was a lot to take in for Luke and me and there were a number of occasions later on when we had to refer to Youtube as a reminder of how to conduct some of the exercises. Despite a long and thoroughly enjoyable career playing club rugby, I was never one for spending time in the gym. I could play an hour and a half of touch rugby without blinking an eye, but the prospect of going for a twenty minute run would fill me with dread and I simply wouldn't bother. Now I was trying to support Luke in an environment which was quite unfamiliar and involving a language quite foreign: hip crossover, prayer stretch, inchworm, thoracic stretch, banded monster walks, banded rotations, mini banded wall walks - that was just the warm-ups!

This new phase had certainly reinvigorated Luke's drive and enthusiasm for all the rehab work he had to do. This had been an important year in Luke's academic life. He had been revising for his GCSE exams and certainly during the summer term had found it increasingly difficult to balance the rehab with the revision. Occasionally the revision took precedent and his rehab work was placed on the backburner. I could understand that and it was encouraging to see Luke taking his exams so seriously. He knew like the rest of us how important a good crop of GCSE results could be with regards to university applications a few years down the line. However, with the GCSE exams now behind him and an injection of rejuvenated enthusiasm and excitement with this new program provided by Mr Satt, he seemed back on track. He was as determined as ever to place himself in the best possible physical condition to return to playing rugby with real confidence.

We had a few sessions in the school gym before leaving for our summer family holiday to Tenerife. We were going to a decent resort which, on the website at least, boasted a plush fitness suite. It wasn't clear therefore to what extent Luke would be able to continue his strength and conditioning. Luke had been joined in the school gym by his brother Matthew, who was now back from the University of Durham. It was good that the pair of them were training together. On arrival therefore at the resort, we all tracked down the gym and began working through the machines to identify which of the exercises on Joe's program we could continue with and which we couldn't. For the most part we got lucky, but the most significant hindrance was the lack of an adjustable machine that would allow Luke to continue with his neck loading. As it turned out, between us, we had forgotten the head harness in any event. I would have been doubly frustrated had there been an adjustable machine on which Luke could work in the knowledge that the harness was still hung up on the hook in our hallway at home! I had taken the clipboard with Joe's program and three times a week during our stay, we meticulously worked our way through the sessions. They were hard work for Luke. I recall on the first couple of occasions he was in a lot of discomfort from some severe sunburn on his belly upon which the top of the shorts was rubbing during many of the exercises. He persevered though and, even on the days when he'd been splashing around in the pool for long periods, he got stuck into his gym work in the late afternoon.

We were also aware at this point, that later in August, Luke was pencilled in for an adenoidectomy. We had found out about a year before that Luke had never been able to breathe properly through his nose! Memories of him as a young boy with his mouth permanently open and dribble pouring down his chin and onto his chest came flooding back and it all seemed to make sense. I remember chatting with Celeste during that period when he was very young, wondering at what point he would grow out of his dribbling. "Surely he won't continue dribbling into his twenties?" I remember saying jokingly. The plan had been for the NHS to remove his adenoids under general anaesthetic the summer before, but of course his injury and subsequent surgery in Argentina wrote off that plan. We had to begin the process all over again with visits to the GP, referrals and appointments at the Lister Hospital in Stevenage. Now we knew that on 8th August he would be having this procedure and the inevitable 7 to 10 days of rest and recovery afterwards. It was important therefore during this last phase of his rehab that we couldn't waste the two weeks in Tenerife; fair play to Luke therefore, he certainly did not.

On our return from our holiday, it became important for us to try to see Jonathan before Luke's adenoid operation. That way, we would have a clear program in place for Luke's last month, which we could begin as soon as Luke felt able to after recovering from having his adenoids out. Jonathan was very busy with Saracens in the middle of their pre-season schedule, but he was kind enough to see us at short notice the day before Luke's operation. We marched over to the

Saracens gym and Luke, after a short warm-up, was strapped in to the measuring gauge to see what progress he had made on his neck strength. Jonathan was particularly keen to identify if Luke had made some ground with addressing the imbalance of the ratio between flexion and extension that had been highlighted at the previous visit. Luke pulled away with his head at this gadget in all four directions. Jonathan calculated his progress and as he was investigating the flexion/extension ratio he told me "we are looking for about 3/5". He showed me his calculator and I was overjoyed to see the result: 60.08%. "That's spot-on," said Jonathan. We then returned to Jonathan's office to discuss a final program which would see Luke slowly but steadily return to full contact and live scrummaging.

Luke would first get used to hitting a tackle sausage at walking pace using one shoulder then the next with the emphasis being on control and building confidence. He would know which shoulder he would use. When he felt comfortable, he would increase the speed of the collision but still very much under his own control before bringing in a late decision as to which shoulder to use. With the decision-making process he would return to a walking pace and then once again build from there. Next was a progression to a tackle shield and then a person using the same controlled process as for the tackle sausage. Breakdown work would also be practised using the same systematic progressions. Luke was expecting to play in the front row despite being nearly 6'4" which of course was a great matter of concern to parents but we had to be guided by Jonathan's considerable experience and confidence in Luke's physical progress. The suggestion was that to begin with he would simply lean into the scrum machine on his own in order to get comfortable and get used to the feel of it again. He would then lean in and begin pushing before progressing to a scrum hit into the machine and then a hit and push. This incremental process was carefully thought through and at each stage allowed Luke the decision-making responsibility to move on. That process could then be restarted by including another member of the front row before starting the third time with a full front row. It was a deliberately structured process. The next stage would be to add in a second row, then a number eight, before starting the whole process again with the addition of flankers to make up a full pack. It was a lot to take on board and it wasn't clear initially how long it would take Luke to make his way through the progression.

While we were waiting for Luke to reappear after having his adenoids cut out under general anaesthetic, I had a conversation with his GP requesting one final x-ray. We were now only weeks away from a potential return to playing rugby and I was keen to put in place as many layers of reassurance as I could. The reassurance was largely for his parents' benefit, but this would also allow Luke to return with as much confidence as possible. I was as aware as anybody that if Luke returned to contact rugby in a half-hearted manner, due to a lack of confidence, this was most likely to end in further injury. His GP was initially reluctant to accommodate our request. "Is he in any pain?" he asked, to which I could only reply "no". The doctor went on, "Is he experiencing any neurological symptoms?" Once again my reply was "no". Under normal circumstances, a request for an x-ray for what appeared to be a perfectly healthy neck would simply not be entertained. However, after a short discussion, the GP did understand where I was coming from and referred us for an x-ray. Later that day, Celeste and I had the great joy to hear the words "I can breathe through my nose" from an albeit slightly groggy son, recovering from his second operation in 12 months.

It didn't take long to get the x-ray completed but my plan backfired slightly when I read the radiologist's report. Although it suggested that the fusion had been a success, it went on to suggest that a CT scan could confirm that and also said in black-and-white, that the consultant should give clearance before returning to playing rugby. I have to admit that my heart sank as I had visions of us waiting several weeks before getting an appointment with a consultant. I felt incredibly sorry for Luke. After all his efforts, the beginning of the season would come and go and he would be left hanging, knowing that he was perfectly able to begin playing, but he would have to endure the frustration of waiting for a thumbs up from a consultant he might not see for weeks. It was doubly frustrating as Jonathan George had already confirmed Luke as being ready to play again. In fact, I had even managed to forward a copy of this last x-ray to Mr Terraza, his surgeon back in Mendoza. He also confirmed that the process had been a success and was delighted that Luke could play rugby again. I made phone calls, I sent letters and I urged our GP to weave some magic to hurry along the referral. In the first bit of bad luck for some time, our consultant Mr Ahmed, was on holiday! I took the decision to arrange a private consultation with Mr Ahmed on his return. I was prepared to pay the extra money not to have to watch Luke waiting any longer.

In the interim period, Luke returned to Hertford Rugby Club and got involved in a training session, his first at the club since his injury. We were still at this point, at the end of the summer holidays. Despite the fact that there were very few players present (the vast majority were having a good time at the Reading Festival!!), Luke trained with the obvious enthusiasm of someone enjoying his rugby for the first time in over a year! He had a good session and didn't appear the slightest bit rusty. Later that week, Luke also completed the last of his scheduled gym sessions that the strength and conditioning coach Joe Satt had programmed. He could now look forward to simply joining the rest of the group with their S & C program; another step in the direction of normality. On that occasion, after completing his last gym session he met up with one of his friends, Wihan, to kick a ball around on the playing fields. According to Luke, he successfully kicked a goal from the halfway line and by chance, Michael Owen, the Director of Rugby at Haileybury was passing by and refused to believe Luke had achieved such a feat. When Luke returned home that day he was very quick to tell me that not only had he kicked a goal from the halfway line but that he had repeated the feat in front of Michael Owen in order to prove that he could. These were the actions of a young man overflowing with raw enthusiasm for playing rugby again.

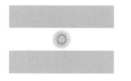 

The Return

A very kind lady operating the phones at the Rivers Hospital in Sawbridgeworth, whose name now escapes me, was incredibly helpful in organising a prompt appointment with Mr Ahmed as soon as he returned from holiday. There seemed to be some confusion or uncertainty as to whether Mr Ahmed would be able to get hold of the x-ray image prior to our appointment. I sent all manner of emails and attempted scans, but in the end I believe this nice lady was able to extrapolate the image from the NHS system. I drove Luke to the consultation full of optimism and high expectations though throughout, I was nagged by an irritating thought that this would cost me £250! We arrived at this private hospital, were greeted with a smile and a couple of forms to fill in. These were largely involved with documenting our insurance scenario or indeed if we were paying privately. We were! Argh!

We waited for no longer than about seven minutes before the familiar and kind face of Mr Ahmed appeared in the corridor. He greeted us warmly with handshakes and invited us to his consultation room. He explained that he was about to clear with our GP that Luke could return to rugby, that he was entirely satisfied with the x-ray image, the growth of new bone fusing the three vertebrae in question and that so long as there were no further neurological concerns that Luke could play immediately. He reiterated the importance of continuing with Luke's strength and conditioning but that he could see no reason not to play. We were not in the room longer than eight or nine minutes and Mr Ahmed was kind enough to waive the £250 fee. He struck me as a very decent human being and after a few final pieces of advice we said our goodbyes and walked back to the car feeling terrific.

Due to the delay in seeing the consultant and the whole palaver of reviewing the x-ray, Luke was not able to play in the first game of the season so we made plans around the second fixture. It was a home game against Felsted on a bright, sunny and very hot day in early September. Luke started on the bench for the 2nd XV and would come on for the last 10 minutes. A number of people had made it over to XX Acre to watch including Celeste and his older brother Matthew, who was yet to return to university. I had visions of me becoming extremely emotional as I had been throughout the whole time Luke's story had been unfolding. We had briefed the opposition coach in order for him to keep an eye on Luke as well and of course the referee was very much in the know. When the moment came, having spent most of the second half checking my watch so I wouldn't actually forget to put Luke on (as if that was going to happen!!), finally he was called up and on he went. I was coaching the XXX so I was able to keep a close eye. He bounded onto the pitch to great applause and with real confidence. I think he really enjoyed the moment. His 10 minutes went very quickly, but he was able to make a number of valuable contributions. It wasn't long before he had to pack down for the first scrum and although he didn't break his neck during a scrum this was a nervy moment. We needn't have worried, as he put a devastating shove on his opposite number and the ball was played away after a very solid set piece. Later he burst through the middle of a ruck to affect a very valuable turnover and he worked hard throughout his 10 minutes. I sent a photograph to our friends at LTRC which was immediately shared on their Facebook page resulting in a large number of likes and subsequent comments. It was great sharing that moment with our friends. I hadn't been emotional at all. Perhaps I was simply too pleased for Luke and indeed equally, I believe the sense of satisfaction in having steered him for over a year to this very moment was enough to hold back my tears.

A week later, we had an away game at Oundle. Once again, Luke would begin on the bench but on this occasion he played the whole of the second half. He had another good performance with some good carries and offloads. The week after, the Haileybury 1st XV had a one-off *classic clash* game to be played at the home of Saracens, Allianz Park. Luke was picked for the squad and would go on for a short spell. He had proved himself fit and strong enough at 2nd XV level and the natural progression was to have a short spell at the next level up. The game was not only exciting for us because Luke would be playing for the XV but also he would be playing alongside Manu, our young guest from Mendoza. In addition, the game was being streamed live on YouTube and the folks over at Los Tordos Rugby Club would be watching. There was much excitement therefore, on both sides of the Atlantic. The match was a stiff test for Haileybury as the Llandovery team provided a physical challenge matched by top-class skills and a mindset to play ambitious rugby from all areas of the field. In the end the difference between the two sides fell to a long-range penalty goal from one of Luke's teammates, Jack Barnes. A hero moment if ever there was one! Luke ended up having a short spell either side of half-time but returned later in the game to replace an injured teammate. It worked out exactly as I had hoped: his first game for the 1st XV was a significant milestone; the final step in a long journey. That the occasion was marked by an appearance at Allianz Park was a huge enhancement of the moment and made the event all the more memorable. The icing on the cake on a more personal level was him playing alongside Manu, a representative from Los Tordos Rugby Club, the club who had taken such care over Luke and me just over a year before. At one point Luke packed down next to Manu in the front row and I was able to take a half decent photograph which I later posted on the LTRC Facebook page. The game was watched by many people over in Argentina on the live stream on YouTube. In addition, there was a huge amount of interest and reaction to the photograph I took of Manu and Luke, bound and crouching side-by-side prior to a scrum. For me, one example stood out above the rest. It was a comment from Pancho, the man who had done so much at the hospital to engage the wheels of progress in terms of getting the insurance company to guarantee payment for the major surgery Luke needed, to repair his broken neck.

It simply read: "It's hard to believe."

<u>The Warm Down</u>

For me, this story is based on fortune … luck. Firstly, Luke had the bad fortune of mistiming a tackle and getting himself into an awkward position, which led to him fracturing one of his vertebrae and injuring his spinal cord. From that moment on, as he lay alone and motionless on the grass of the first team pitch at Los Tordos Rugby Club, in Mendoza, Argentina, his fortunes changed immediately. From there on in, he was to benefit from nothing but good luck, manifesting itself largely in the actions of good, decent human beings. For example, the swift appearance of the club doctor, Peco, and his decisive actions. In addition, coming across the good people of LTRC whose instinctive display of rugby spirit was so much in evidence and whose supportive and empathetic approach to looking after us has meant we have new friends and family for life; strong bonds based on human responses to near catastrophic conditions, resulting in success and happiness.

Was it good luck that the touring company had scheduled LTRC for the fixture that day? Was it good luck that Luke injured himself during one of our two club games rather than one of the two school games? Was it good luck that the injury occurred during the same week the Pumas were playing South Africa, in Mendoza? The elements of luck in this story are clear and obvious; however, they are entirely underpinned by the actions of kind people and most vitally, how these actions affected Luke.

Our father and son relationship will never be the same again. Luke and I were given an unusual opportunity, forced as we were, in less than ideal circumstances, to spend more time together than would ordinarily be the case. In fact, for several days we were together permanently. The early days of no Wi-Fi brought us closer and Luke's highly dependent situation, unable to move for days as he was, felt like turning back the clocks; like having a baby again. But he didn't stay in that condition long and just like when he was a baby, I was able to relive his progress, albeit in short steps, from total dependence to increasing levels of independence and eventually total independence and a return to playing rugby. It was as if I was watching his life starting all over again but watching it in *fast forward*. It was a complete joy to watch him grow in strength and confidence, to witness a young man, still a child in many respects, approaching his circumstances philosophically, calmly but with an air of determination, fuelled by a clear goal: to play again.

Over the months, I developed a huge amount of respect for my son and I could not be more proud of what he achieved in what ended up being a little over a year of his life. His story is inspirational not least as it played out during an important academic year for him, taking on his GCSE exams. That he ended up with a splendid set of results is also testament to his strength of character and determination. To have managed a long period of rest, estranged as he was from the sporting endeavours that he loved so much, showed great patience and when the time came to begin his rehab, he displayed great discipline and determination for a young man of his age. Months of visits to the gym several times a week, alongside exercises in his bedroom in the evenings and putting up with the constant frustration of seeing his buddies enjoying their sport all added to his growth and development as a person. He knows now that the hard work is not over. Now that he is a member of Haileybury's 1st XV, the strength and conditioning will remain a part of his routine and the ghastly neck loading that is so difficult to watch, as he strains every sinew in his neck must continue for ever, if he wishes to continue playing rugby. But playing rugby was his goal and this is what drove him throughout that difficult time. It is what he loves doing and I understand that perfectly having enjoyed a long club career myself. It reminds me of the words of Haileybury's most recent international rugby player, Kapeliele Pifeleti, who was a boarder in my house, Lawrence. He was recently capped by the USA Eagles and, in fact, also just played his first premiership game for Saracens. I know that, as I once promised him I would come and watch his debut for Sarries and Luke and I saw him just a few days ago as I write. KP, as we know him, was also subject to an unforgettable gesture of rugby camaraderie during his time at school, which I think is worth sharing. He was a rugby scholar from Tonga and after arriving at Haileybury for the sixth form, had not seen his mother for two years. The then captain of the XV, Ed Harris, arranged for the players to club together, behind KP's back, and buy his mother a plane ticket to the UK to watch their game against Eton, due to be played later that month at Allianz Park. At the last training session before the game, a car pulled up at the ground and his mother stepped out! Everyone there knew what was happening except KP. "Oh! That's my Mom!" he said, startled and visibly moved. There was not a dry eye to be seen as the boys clapped and watched him hugging his Mum. Unforgettable scenes!

So I once asked KP for his favourite quote to put on a notice outside his boarding room. He told me he'd like the quote, "Do the mahi, get the treats" on his sheet. KP explained to me that *mahi* meant hard work in Tongan.

Luke did the *mahi*. His treat? He's playing rugby again.

Above: My Dad, me and Luke during our memorable day
as guests of the RFU IPF. Below: Ready for Luke's first day
back at school.

The game really should have finished a draw!

After months of total rest, patience and no small amount of frustration, Luke was finally allowed to begin his path to recovery. This was his first session in the gym.

Above: His first game back: the last 10 minutes for the XXX
(2nd XV).

Below: Two weeks later, Luke's first game for the XV,
packing down next to Manu at Allianz Park.

The early stages of the neck loading – just 5 kgs at this point.

Juan Figallo visiting Luke at school.

Luke and Jonathan George after his final session with the
Saracens physio.

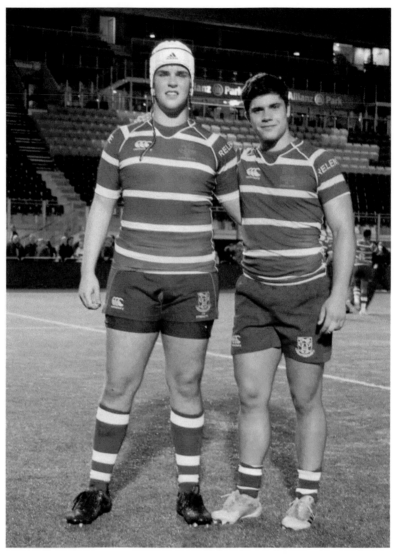

For Luke to have made his 1st XV debut in such extraordinary circumstances was a wonderful way to close out the story. That Manu from LTRC was by his side was the icing on the cake!

Messages From Home

From the moment word began to spread amongst my friends and colleagues, the messages began to pour in. A mixture of texts and emails, all communicating the deepest concern, were channelled through my phone. During the most worrying moments, I would sit and read…and re-read these. Sat in a hospital room for hours during the day, I really looked forward to exchanges on WhatsApp and other platforms. Just to connect with others, who were displaying such tremendous care for Luke, was a tonic in itself. I felt less alone…

Messages of Support

<u>Email: Monday 20th August 2018 from Martin Collier, The Master of Haileybury:</u>

"Dear Carl

Angus has emailed me to inform me of Luke's injury. I hope that Luke is comfortable and that you and he are bearing up in the circumstances. The situation must be very difficult for you; if there is anything which I can do to help you in any way, please do not hesitate to get in touch.

Please pass my regards to Luke.

Yours

Martin"

<u>Email: Wednesday 22nd August 2018 from Alan Pilgrim, Haileybury's Chairman of Governers:</u>

"Carl

Martin told me about Luke's serious injury. I do hope he is getting the best of care and that the operation goes well.

If there is anything the school can do please let Martin know. Everyone is thinking of you and your family.

Warm regards

Alan"

Email: Thursday 23rd August 2018 from my newly appointed Head of House elect, Sam Hurding:

"Sir,

I hope that Luke is recovering well and is feeling better. Tour has felt different without him and yourself.

If you need anything done or brought in for yourself and your family and especially Luke please email me or my parents we will be glad to help.

Yours sincerely,

Sam"

Email: Thursday 23rd August 2018 from Chris Lowe, a former Lawrence boy and member of Haileybury's Council of Governers:

"Hi Carl

Just heard about Luke. Obviously a matter of great concern. Martin suggests all should ultimately be well but this is clearly a very difficult time for him and for you and for all his family.

I look forward to glad tidings in due course but please there is no need to reply. You have greater priorities.

My warmest wishes

Chris"

<u>Text: 24th August 2018 from my good friend Kingsley Wheaton:</u>

"One quick message "off the grid"... Anything you need AT ALL just let me know and we'll do all we can to help... Don't hesitate, you know that, right???? With all our love (just briefed Jules and she was absolutely shocked of course)... Kings, Jules and Co... Xxx"

<u>Text: 26th August 2018 from Andrew Searson, Director of Sport at Haileybury:</u>

"Hi mate. Just heard about Luke's injury. I sincerely hope all is as good as it can be. Let me know if there's anything I can do. Thinking of you all mate. Andy"

<u>Texts: 20th August – 4th September 2018 from Darron Moore, Luke's coach at Hertford RFC:</u>

"Don't know what to say
Completely shocked if there is anything we can do just ask. All our love to you all."

"Just don't know what to say mate

Does he still have feeling in his legs?"

"Send him all our love from all the under 16's A speedy recovery and a very safe journey home"

"Thinking of you both"

"Hope he is recovering well. All our best wishes, the Moores"

<u>Texts: 20th August – 4th September 2018 from John McGurk, Luke's coach at Hertford RFC and father of friend Callum McGurk:</u>

"Hi Carl. I've just heard from Callum that Luke has fractured his vertebra. I'm really sorry to hear this. I hope he will be ok and is not in too much pain. Please wish him well from us. Do let me know how he is getting on. John"

"Fingers crossed for a successful op. Will be thinking of you. Let us know how it goes."

"Hi Carl. Just wondering how you are and how Luke is doing. Has he had his op yet? Hope it goes well and he isn't in too much pain. John"

"Carl just seen your message re the op. That is good news and must be a great relief for you. The main thing is he will recover fully. Give him my regards and safe trip home. Will lookout for you at school. Guess you will be a few weeks before flying back."

"Carl. Hope you don't mind me texting. Jo Moore has contacted me because the rumours have started. She wants to put a note out to Hertford boys to tell them Luke damaged his neck playing and has had a successful op to stabilise his vertebrae and will be flying home in a week or so. Are you happy for something like this to go out? If so do you want to add change or draft something? Or would you prefer she didn't say anything? John"

"Carl it's fantastic the local club have rallied round to support you both. Just shows the best of the rugby fraternity."

"I have been wondering about how he will react. My thoughts for what it's worth are that he has two things to focus on in the immediate future. One is getting better and the other I would say is his GCSEs. Once through this year then there will be time to consider what he will do to fill his time."

"Carl. Rachael has been in tears here too. You don't need me to tell you this and it is what I keep telling Rachael whilst you would never want this sort of thing to happen, it is a good news story as he is going to be fine got full movement. We will give him all the support he needs to get over this and find something to fill the void as long as it isn't Xbox! Stay strong."

"How's mum? Let me know if you need me to do anything"

"Carl. Seen the video of Luke up and walking. Looking good. When do you fly back? Let me know if you want me to meet you and bring you back."

"Hi Carl just wondering how you are getting on. Saw the video of Luke walking which was great to see. Any news on when you are flying back? Let me know if you would like me to pick you up. John"

"Hi Carl. Hope you are well and back into the swing of things. Just wondering how Luke is doing hope to see him around school sometime. John"

<u>Texts: 22th August – 21st September 2018 from Jamie Hunter, father of team mate at Hertford RFC, Freddie Hunter:</u>

"Please pass on our regards to Luke. Hope you are coping too. Cheers, Jamie and Freddie."

"Very pleased to hear he's on the mend. Real shame about his rugby career though. He has some genuine talent. Take it easy."

"How's Luke getting on? On the mend I hope."

<u>Texts: 20th August – 25th August 2018 from Angus Head, Deputy Head (Co-curricular) of Haileybury:</u>

"Hi Carl. Angus has updated me on Luke's injury. I am so very sorry for him. It must be tremendously stressful for you both. I won't mention anything to Celeste or anyone else here until you say the word. Please keep me updated with progress and let me know if/when/how I can help. So very sorry mate. Hope you are ok too. Angus"

"Good idea. Get some sleep. Let's be in contact later."

"Thanks for the update. Do try to get some sleep. Who is organising the repatriation and when is that likely to be? Will let the people you mention know."

"Ok. Thanks. Have you got anywhere to stay?"

"Sounds like fabulous hosting. I've spoken to Martin this evening. He has emailed you and sends his very best wishes. Do keep me updated please and know that we are all thinking about you and

Luke a great deal. Lots and lots of well-wishers from this side of the world. Hang on in there buddy."

"One step ahead pal. Tracey was with her (Celeste) last night and I've been over and spoken with both Celeste and Matthew this evening. They're ok."

"Hope it's ok to have given Briggsy your number and let him know (without details) what's happened."

"Jesus. Ok, well sounds like good news about the op. I've spoken to Angus about the financial issues. Now resolved. Bad news about the 10 days. Just got to take it day by day I guess. Also, excellent news about Luke walking to the toilet. Hope you can get a bit more sleep tonight. Can I help at all with the Lawrence GCSE results on Thursday maybe? Is someone around to field questions? Happy to advise etc… if need be."

"Spoke to Stephen today. He'll deal with any issues. I don't think there are any. I'm on hand too. Happy to talk to/advise any parents or boys if need be. Hope all goes well tonight. Thinking of you both."

"OK. Well good luck with it all. If that is the right thing to say. Let's communicate again tomorrow. Tracey was with C this afternoon."

"Hi Carl. Any update for today. I saw the photos of the three Pumas. How wonderful. Martin is asking me for regular updates so if there is anything to report please do pass it on. Thanks pal."

"Wonderful news. What a relief."

<u>Transcript of a voicemail left by Dr Bruno Schmir who was the first person to treat Luke on the pitch the day of the injury: 25th August 2018:</u>

"Hello Carl, how you? I am Bruno, people call me Peco, I am the Doctor that make the first attentions to Luke when he was in the match, in the rugby match. Okay I just want to talk to you, to send this message. First of all, sorry for my English, it's very bad, I think I need to take some classes. In second place, I want to say that I am proud because of the evolution of Luke. I went to the hospital, I visit him, you were eating with Juan Aliaga. I was talking with your son and he's a very good boy, he is very strong, I know he will be very good of healthy and also it will be a very good person, he is a good person but he will be a very good man in his life. So congratulations for you, for the son that you have. I talk with him, like half an hour and I saw that he was an special people so at this moment I'm out of Mendoza I'm going to Tucuman that is another province in Argentina. I can't go to visit him. I really want to do but I can't. I can't do because I'm in a trip. So okay that's all. Sorry for my English, I send ahead for you my best wishes and okay it was very nice to meet you, honestly I prefer not to be in this occasion but this is the thing, I don't know, the life or God put in this moment of our lives and all is all right thanks God so nice to meet you Carl and give to Luke my regards please and please if you can send me his contact because I want to make a salute for him too."

<u>Hand written letter to Luke from his former housemaster, Matt Radley dated 29th July 2018:</u>

"Dear Luke,

Like so many people I was terribly shocked and upset to hear of the injury you suffered while on tour. To be injured as you were so far from home must have been an incredibly difficult experience, although I am sure it was a relief that dad was there with you.

It does, however, sound like you received absolutely first rate medical care, and I hear the prognosis is good for your recovery, which is really wonderful to hear. I also gather that you became a bit of a celebrity too, and I even saw a photo of you with some of the Argentinian rugby team!

I am not sure if it is any kind of solace at this stage, but the way in which the rugby community rallied around you and your dad was incredibly heart-warming and, as the saying goes, helps to restore one's faith in humanity a little. The sport which you and I love so much is a global community of really good people, and that spirit is so important and must never be allowed to die. I wish you all the best for a speedy and full recovery, and will be sending good vibes from down here in Devon.

All the very best.

Mr Radley."

Post Scriptum

On completing this book, the months began to pass and as they say, "life moves on." Luke went on to enjoy some of the football season, playing in goal for the College's 2nd XI until further frustration, when a shoulder injury ruled him out of most of the second half of term. For months, the devastation of coronavirus swept across the world from the East, slowly but surely making its way to Europe and the UK. Eventually, on 18 March 2020, Haileybury closed and the dreaded lockdown began. However, the relationship with LTRC, in Mendoza, Argentina, had continued to develop. The friendships born from Luke's near catastrophic injury and the success story of his recovery that ensued had remained strong, despite the long distances and separation involved. Plans had been put in place to invite two of our sixth form Spanish students to spend a few weeks in the summer, honing their language skills with families from Los Tordos. In addition, the rugby club was also in the process of selecting two further young ambassadors to join Haileybury in September. Such was the success of the visit of Manu and Santi the previous year, borne largely of the outstanding impression they had left, the Master was keen to repeat the arrangement year on year. The promise of reciprocal invitations for our Spanish students going forward, was building the foundations of a genuine exchange programme. I had also hoped that at some point during this summer, I might fly to Mendoza for a few weeks and assist with coaching rugby, in some small and very personal way, making a contribution of thanks for their care and support in 2018. Sadly, COVID-19 is likely to ruin our plans albeit temporarily. As I write, the virus is making its way through South America with no small amount of devastation and it is my heartfelt hope that our new friends in Argentina are spared the worst of this awful pandemic.

I hope that before not too long, they will be able to reunite back at their club, at first no doubt, for administrative purposes but then, before not too long, and as restrictions relax, to resume their incredible social atmosphere, where they can continue to mould such fantastic young people, within the rugby-playing environment.

Luke and I have decided to provide Los Tordos Rugby Club with a trophy. It is our hope that this trophy will be awarded annually to a young player, boy or girl, of any age, who has overcome some kind of difficulty or challenge. This could be an injury, illness, bereavement or some other mental or physical hurdle that has required that young person to show resilience, determination and maturity beyond their years to conquer their challenge. Luke and I of course, would be equally delighted if the trophy never has to be awarded at all, for obvious reasons!

So we look forward in the future to many happy years of collaborating with our new friends in Mendoza, recognising that our young people have much to learn from a rich variety of experience on both sides of the Atlantic.

It has been a hugely therapeutic exercise writing this book and it gives me great satisfaction to donate my royalties to the RFU Injured Players Foundation. Therefore thank you for your contribution in purchasing a copy.